DANIEL O'CONNELL

Political Pioneer

DANIEL O'CONNELL

Political Pioneer

Edited by
Maurice R. O'Connell

Institute of Public Administration
on behalf of
DOCAL—Daniel O'Connell Association Ltd

First published in 1991 on behalf of
DOCAL—Daniel O'Connell Association Ltd
by the
Institute of Public Administration
57-61 Lansdowne Road
Dublin 4
Ireland

British Library Cataloguing in Publication Data

Daniel O'Connell: Political Pioneer
  I. O'Connell, Maurice R. (Maurice Richard)
  941.5081092

  ISBN 1 872002 11 0

Cover portrait of Daniel O'Connell by Count Alfred d'Orsay,
circa 1830, from the drawing-room at Derrynane.

Cover and illustrations designed by Butler Claffey Design, Dún Laoghaire
Typeset in 10/12 Palatino by Wendy A. Commins, The Curragh
Printed by Colour Books, Dublin

CONTENTS

CONTRIBUTORS

Peter Alter is Deputy Director of the German Historical Institute, London

Paddy Bushe, Waterville, Co. Kerry, is the author of *Poems with Amergin* (Dublin, 1989)

Tom Garvin is Professor of Politics at University College Dublin

Brian Girvin is a Lecturer in the Department of Modern History, University College Cork

Geraldine Grogan, Dublin, is the author of *The Noblest Agitator: Daniel O'Connell and the German Catholic Movement 1830-1850* (Dublin, 1991)

Pierre Joannon is Honorary Consul General of Ireland in the South of France and editor of the journal *Etudes Irlandaises*

Joseph Lee is Professor of Modern History at University College Cork

James N. McCord is Professor of History at the College of William and Mary, Williamsburg, Virginia

Fergus O'Ferrall, Dublin, is the author of *Catholic Emancipation: Daniel O'Connell and the Birth of Irish Democracy 1820-30* (Dublin, 1985)

Diarmaid Ó Muirithe is a Lecturer in the Department of Modern Irish Language and Literature, University College Dublin

PREFACE

This book is the published form of the papers read last October at the Daniel O'Connell Association's Workshop at the Derrynane Hotel, close to O'Connell's ancestral home.

The Association aims to stimulate thinking towards a national philosophy for a fully-developed democratic Ireland in a uniting Europe; and in particular to explore the nature of the Irish state and how best to realise its potentialities. The Association see O'Connell as having established the tradition of democracy in Ireland, and they wish to investigate the extent to which his ideas and example may be relevant to the development of modern Ireland.

In my work as editor I owe a debt of gratitude to the members of the Association, and in particular to its chairman, Tom Barrington.

I should also like to thank Jim O'Donnell, head of the Publishing Division of the Institute of Public Administration, and three members of its staff — Kathleen Harte, Iain MacAulay and Finbarr O'Shea.

The enthusiasm shown by the members of the Association and by the public attending the Workshop is an encouragement to the Organising Committee in its continuing work.

Maurice R. O'Connell
Editor
September 1991

1

DANIEL O'CONNELL

J.J. Lee

The main events of O'Connell's career can be quickly summarised. He was born on 6 August 1775 at Carhen, near Cahirciveen, Co. Kerry, in the extreme south-west of Ireland. He died on 15 May 1847 in Genoa. He was educated successively from 1791 until 1798 in St Omer, Douai, London and Dublin, where he was called to the Bar. He founded the Catholic Association in 1823, and his victory in the Clare by-election in 1828 led to Catholic Emancipation in 1829. From then until his death, he played a prominent role in parliamentary as well as popular politics. He became the first Catholic Lord Mayor of the reformed corporation of Dublin in 1841, but he failed to achieve his main goal, Repeal of the Act of Union. The decision of the Prime Minister, Sir Robert Peel, to mobilise superior British military power to resist Repeal in 1843 exposed the fundamental weakness of a constitutional (or indeed insurrectionary) movement confronted by resolute military force. Although criticised in abstract terms by Young Ireland ideologists in 1846 for his opposition to violence in principle, he retained overwhelming popular support. But his health deteriorated sadly, and he was on a pilgrimage to Rome, in the hope of both physical and spiritual succour, when he died at Genoa.

O'Connell lived through a period of extraordinary social, cultural and political turmoil. His life broadly spanned the age of the Industrial Revolution in England. In Ireland it coincided with an unprecedented

1

growth of population, which more than doubled between 1775 and 1845. The last two years of O'Connell's life were overshadowed by the Great Famine, the most catastrophic experience in western Europe in several centuries, which claimed at least a million dead, and during which another million emigrated, between 1845 and 1850.

Social and demographic change coincided with a period of seminal cultural change. O'Connell lived through one of the most dramatic language shifts recorded in modern European history. Born into a family of Gaelic-speaking landlords, still in close communion with an ancient Gaelic culture, he would watch that culture collapse in the course of his lifetime as the Irish language succumbed to the superior socio-political power of English.

O'Connell both witnessed and promoted dramatic political change. A student in France at the time of the Revolution, its atrocities would leave an indelible impression on his mind, inclining him to a position close to pacificism. In 1800 he vigorously opposed the abolition of the Irish parliament, and Ireland's effective annexation by Britain through the Act of Union. In the course of his campaigns for Catholic Emancipation and for Repeal of the Union he pioneered the creation of a modern political party and vastly extended the role of popular politics, not only by Irish, but by international standards.

His public life was spent mainly in opposition. By profession a lawyer, he won national renown for the skill and audacity of his defence of the poor against the power of the state machine. In popular imagination, O'Connell was the defender of downtrodden Catholics in a game which had to be played by enemy rules, and in which therefore the rules were made to be broken. So brightly did his reputation shine in this respect, and so long did it survive, that as late as 1949 a candidate in the West Donegal by-election could find himself extolled as "a wizard, a modern Dan O'Connell, for he has so manipulated the technicalities of law that he has had cases dismissed for defendants who had actually admitted their guilt".

So completely did O'Connell come to incarnate a people that his popular image often bore little relation to reality. It is the fortune or the fate of charismatic heroes to have projected onto them the suppressed self-images of their followers. Gaelic folk-heroes had rendered a psychic service to the vivid imagination of the plain people by having attributed to them tales of insatiable sexual prowess. It is a tribute to O'Connell's popular stature that he was the first in centuries to adequately service the popular imagination in this respect. As far as the evidence goes, there was no basis for the attribution. In 1802, he risked disinheritance — and actually suffered it for three years — by his rich and financially calculating uncle, in order to marry his wife, Mary, for love. He remained devoted to her, and was distraught on her death in 1836. The stories of O'Connell's philandering tell us far more about the need of the popular imagination than they do about the historic O'Connell.

His legendary exploits as a defence lawyer won him the national accolade of "The Counsellor O'Connell" even before he came to be called the Liberator for his role in Catholic Emancipation. In parliament too, he found himself more often in opposition to the government than in alliance with it. But, coming to Westminster at the relatively late age of fifty-four, he nevertheless established his authority as one of the outstanding parliamentarians, and the outstanding parliamentary radical, of his generation. And indefatigable though he was in pursuing what he saw as Irish interests, his contribution to parliament was by no means confined to Irish issues. He was recognised as a statesman of the highest stature. His opinions commanded interest throughout Europe, America and Latin America, in a manner unrivalled by the views of any other Irish political figure before or since.

This is not to imply that other Irish political figures did not occasionally rouse international interest. Charles Stewart Parnell and Eamon de Valera became widely known for their contribution to the national independence struggle and as representatives of the will to freedom of a suppressed people. Michael Collins, in addition, was a name to conjure with, for students of guerilla tactics. These were no mean distinctions, and I do not wish in any way to disparage them. Nevertheless, it is a simple historical fact that O'Connell's career aroused wider international interest than that of any other figure in Irish public life.

Part of the wider European interest in O'Connell, it ought to be stressed, did derive from the fact that Ireland was then a country of some significance, for two reasons which no longer apply. Firstly, it was part of the United Kingdom, then the most advanced and most powerful state in the world. Therefore any major political movement within the UK became a matter of much higher international significance than today. Secondly, Ireland was not then the miniscule country in population terms that it is now. We have to keep reminding ourselves how Ireland's population has fallen not only in absolute but, even more strikingly, in relative terms since O'Connell's time. In 1840, for instance, its more than 8 million people far outnumbered Belgium's 4 million, Sweden's 3.1 million, Holland's 2.9, Scotland's 2.6, Switzerland's 2.2, Finland's 1.4, Norway's 1.3, and Denmark's 1.3. England and Wales had of course a bigger population. But with 16 million people, they were only twice as big. Ireland accounted for about one-third of the population of the UK, a far higher proportion than today. It is true that Germany had 30 million people, and Italy 22 million at the time. But Germany and Italy did not then exist as states. (Neither, of course, did Ireland. But everybody realised she was not England.)

3

Ireland had a bigger population than any of the numerous states within the present-day boundaries of Germany and Italy, except for Prussia. The Ireland of O'Connell was poor, but she was not insignificant.

O'Connell was widely acknowledged as the tribune of a rising people, acquiring further recognition from the perception, largely justified, that it was he himself who dragged them at least half way up towards a standing position. But interest in him was greatly intensified by the fact that he was also perceived as representing great principles of universal and enduring import, which incorporated, but transcended, Irish experience.

The famous English historian, Macauley, recorded:

> Go where you will on the Continent, visit any coffee house, dine at any table, embark upon any steam boat, enter any conveyance — from the moment your accent shows you to be an Englishman, the very first question you are asked by your companions, be they advocates, merchants, manufacturers, physicians or peasants like our yeomen, is: "what is to be done with O'Connell?".

Balzac would later recall:

> I would like to have met three men only in this century; Napoleon, Cuvier and O'Connell.

O'Connell's campaign for Catholic Emancipation was rightly seen as an epic battle for civil liberties. It was not only his inspirational leadership, however, but his belief in religious tolerance in principle, and his commitment to the separation of church and state, that attracted the admiration of Liberal Catholics on the Continent. They felt themselves an embattled minority as they strove to reconcile the old ecclesiastical order, with its long tradition of support for autocracy, with liberalism and even with democracy. Those who felt that the Catholic Church would seriously damage itself if it were seen to align with reaction, greeted O'Connell as the man who showed how liberalism was compatible with loyalty to Rome, how democracy and religious devotion could flourish together.

But O'Connell's appeal, powerful though it was for Liberal Catholics, extended far beyond Catholic circles. For O'Connell detested ascendancy in all its forms. Despite all the twists and turns inevitable in the career of a practical politician operating from a position of weakness, obliged to mould his material and ad lib his script as he went along, there is a remarkable consistency in O'Connell's underlying commitment to the principles of civil liberty. His convictions were based on genuine belief, not merely on opportunistic reaction to Irish circumstances. He hated the ascendancy mentality, not only because he equated it with English victimisation of Ireland, or Protestant victimisation of Irish Catholics, but because, as above all a champion of individual liberty, he detested any system that placed one people, one race, one religion, one class, above another. For O'Connell there was no contradiction between an Irish urge to freedom and a universal desire for freedom. If he championed Catholic Emancipation in Ireland, he denounced Spanish persecution of Protestants. He opposed Black slavery, even to the extent of alienating some of his support among Irish Americans, anxious to insist on their own superiority to Blacks. He was a powerful advocate of the emancipation of the Jews, and of Latin American independence, the main "colonial" issue of the day. He was too, in the context of his time, an advanced advocate of women's emancipation. "Mind", he liked to say, "has no sex".

These views naturally roused not only intense admiration, but also bitter resistance. It was ironic that so vigorous a critic of violence should have shown so peculiar a penchant, even by the standards of the time, for verbal violence. The always emphatic, and often vituperative, vocabulary in which he expressed his views forced his listeners and readers to take sides. No one could be neutral on O'Connell. His views on violence provoked some debate at the time, and much more since. His trenchant criticism of violence was based on two beliefs. Firstly, he rejected violence on moral grounds. In his view, violence was itself so evil that no other evil justified its use. Secondly, he felt that violence was counterproductive. Rightly or wrongly, he took the view that it was, by definition, reactionary, because it was bound to consume its children and lead to greater injustices than the ones it rebelled against. He felt that it was more the gravedigger than the midwife of progress. And he was passionately committed to the idea of progress in a Victorian sense.

His relative indifference not only towards the Irish language, but towards cultural diversity in general, continues to provoke intense controversy. Some may even detect an internal contradiction between his detestation of political and professional ascendancy, and his relative indifference to cultural ascendancy.

There were apparent internal contradictions in other respects also, although many of them may at least be understood, if not necessarily condoned, when seen in correct historical context. If ever there was a protean personality, it was O'Connell. He was, on the one hand, a rumbustious puller of strokes, an enthusiastic political manoeuvrer, a rogue, and a fixer. Jobs for the boys, not least his boys, was part of both the Gaelic culture from which he sprang, and the parliamentary culture to which he gravitated. But by the standards of the time, he could also be considered a proponent of an enterprise culture. Yet, although a strong believer in individual initiative, he also cared passionately about the poor, and sought to protect them from the predatory impulses of the rich. Although a strong critic of certain aspects of contemporary craft unionism, particularly of the exclusive and violent Dublin type, he indulged no illusions of the "greed is good" variety. Just as he straddled different political cultures, so he straddled different mentalities. Identifying and explaining the contradictions as well as the consistencies in O'Connell remains a subject of absorbing historical enquiry.

2

O'CONNELL AND THE
MAKING OF IRISH POLITICAL
CULTURE

Tom Garvin

A CULTURE DENIED POLITICS: IRELAND
1690-1823

Daniel O'Connell grew up in a country which lacked any tradition of democratic or even quasi-democratic self-government. One of the greatest tragedies of Irish political development was the weakness, unique in western Europe, of civic tradition. This weakness was, of course, not the fault of the population itself, but rather of the settlement of 1690, which ensured a permanent divorce between the great majority of the population and those who owned the land of Ireland. In some of the major European states, a somewhat similar destruction of mediaeval representative civic institutions had occurred because of the centralising effects of absolutism; Montesquieu's critique of French government bears adequate witness.

In Ireland, due in part to the overwhelming weight of English power in the remaking of Ireland after 1690, domestic political life became almost non-existent; the Dublin parliament of the eighteenth century was unrepresentative of the population, like other European parliaments; it was also commonly required by London to govern, or rather to witness

7

London's governing, against the interests of those few whom it did represent. Rather like soi-disant representative government in Brezhnev's Soviet Union, politics in pre-1823 Ireland was a perverse parody of the real thing, even by the standards of that era. Irish people were denied a political life; all this is well-known, but the extraordinary achievement of O'Connell as a political teacher of the people is persistently understated or even denied by many commentators writing subsequent to his death in 1845.

This is not to say that O'Connell and his followers were dealing with a culture which "had no politics". A human culture that has no political component is inconceivable, and only very deranged political theorists would suggest that it is. The denial of a legal political existence to a religious, cultural or racial group amounts to an attempt to deny them politics, and the group will always improvise their own political order, however primitive and distorted, outside the dominant order. Ireland over the past three centuries has continuously generated political "counter-cultures" which are outside the legal political order and which are commonly opposed to that order.[1]

In the period between 1760 and 1847 this political underworld, the product of the imposition of a religious caste system on the island, was at its height. Crucial aspects of this underworld of secret societies, local mafias, committees of enforcement of a local, extra-legal land code and midnight courts were its headlessness and its enormous potential, in certain hands, for violence and even political revolution.

The ideas of the French Revolution of 1789 went through this underworld Ireland like wildfire, and by 1791 a wave of incoherent political mobilisation had occurred among the masses, giving an indication of their political and revolutionary potential to constitutionalists and revolutionaries alike. An American diplomat observed in November 1791:

> This class of people from the revolution in this country, have enjoyed no participation in the Government, nor could they hold long leases of land until within a few years past; the penal laws still exclude them from citizenship. Within a few months [after the Bastille] the Catholics, as if by an electrical impulse, have met in large bodies, and passed resolutions to remain no longer in this excluded state...[there is] a great proportion of respectable rich Catholics at their head...[a refusal to concede repeal of the penal laws] will, according to present appearances, be productive of such a general ferment as Ireland has not experienced for a century past.[2]

He was, of course, prophetic; constitutional action remained impossible, particularly after the recall of Fitzwilliam in 1795, and the mobilisation was taken over by the revolutionaries with catastrophic results in 1798.

O'CONNELL AS REMAKER OF A POLITICAL CULTURE

O'Connell's greatest achievement was to give the mobilising Catholic middle classes, workers and peasantry non-insurrectionist political leadership and transform them into a constitutional political force of great power. His success, although impressive, was incomplete, and the "alternative politics" or insurrectionist tradition in Irish politics lives on even today. However, were it not for O'Connell, the creation of what Jeffrey Praeger has termed a "public space" in Ireland would have been even more difficult than it was in the twentieth century.[3] O'Connell's greatest contribution to the independent Ireland that emerged after 1921 was an ingrained and very widespread, if often inarticulate, hankering after a constitutional order that permitted normal political life, combined with sufficient of the political skills necessary to construct such an order.

In my view, it was a close-run thing, and Latin American-style politics could easily have become dominant. A true tragedy is the weakness of any O'Connell-style political tradition in Northern Ireland.

The submerged peasantry and labourers of eighteenth-century Ireland had evolved a localist political culture that emphasised collective solidarity, the enforcement of folk custom in matters of land-tenancy, marriage, inheritance, support of clergy and relations with landlords. A crude village democracy existed; Whiteboy captains were commonly elected, as were the leaders of factions and hurling teams. In classic Hobbesean fashion, the political state which was denied to them by the Ascendancy tried to create itself at village level in the form of a sort of underworld polity, complete with the functions of judgement and execution.

Willingness to obey folk law was combined with a settled hatred of English law. Absence of true political life generated a debilitating tradition of visionary and millennial political dreaming which is scarcely dead yet. Ireland had no Great Tradition of politics that the common man could feel was his; what he had was a Little Tradition. What O'Connell tried to do was to create a Great Tradition for his people, using his knowledge of the Little Tradition, his Catholicism and his liberalism; in essence, he tried to be Ireland's first democratic law-giver, in appallingly unpromising circumstances. Not only had he to teach the people, he had to teach their priests the practice of electoral democracy; he was less successful in infusing into the Catholic Church democratic philosophical principles. Irish democracy still bears that birthmark, in the form of a strong general understanding of the mechanisms of representative democracy combined ultimately with a disregard for, or unawareness of, the ethical principles that lie behind those mechanics.

Besides O'Connell, two groups of people had toyed with the idea of constructing an alliance with the Catholic masses. These were the Irish Volunteers at the time of the American War, and, of course, the United Irishmen of the 1790s. Both failed, the latter's attempt ending tragically in the massacres of 1798. Richard Lalor Sheil wrote:

> Various schemes of popular organisation had been revolved from time to time in the fertile brain of O'Connell; but that which eventually commended itself above all others to his judgement was one which, while it reserved to persons of better education a controlling power, provided for the involvement of the masses of the people as associate members of the body, the former, on payment of one guinea, and the latter on payment of one shilling a year...The...United Irishmen... afforded an example only to be avoided. [The Volunteers of 1782]...was the improvisation of a national militia by the propertied and privileged classes — [the United Irishmen] the conspiracy of the disenfranchised many.[4]

The new organisation, the first mass political party in the world, would have to

> invite and secure the cooperation of persons of every degree; to win the confidence of the wealthier classes it must avoid every semblance of illegality or enmity to the established order of things; and yet it must, to kindle the smouldering passions of an infuriated and oppressed people, deal fearlessly with those many-sided questions about the opulent and the poor, the well-born and the humble, can seldom, if ever, be expected cordially to agree.[5]

The population had vivid memories of the disaster of 1798, and O'Connell was able to use these memories to persuade the masses to try the road of constitutional agitation. This did not, however, prevent him from appropriating the symbols of the Irish Volunteers for his own, very different movement.

O'CONNELL AS POLITICAL TECHNICIAN

O'Connell's Catholic Association of 1823 was the world's first mass political party, based on a branch system and financed by the tiny but regular contributions (popularly called "rents" in Ireland with delicious irony) of very large numbers of humble people. This kind of political organisation, a commonplace in the West in the late twentieth century, was unprecedented at the time; the Jacobin and Girondin organisations of the French Revolution and the secret caucus organisations of Britain, Ireland and the early United States were not fully-developed voter-directed organisations. "Old Hickory", Jackson's American Democratic Party of 1824, often declared in textbooks to be the first such organisation, was pipped at the historical post by one year by the Irish. Later, of course, Irish emigrants to the United States were to use their political skills, developed in O'Connell's string of political organisations, to take over that very party. In Ireland, Parnell's party, the Gaelic League, the Sinn Féin of 1917-21, Fianna Fáil and Fine Gael are all the unacknow-ledged organisational descendants of O'Connell's party. O'Connell's legacy is not recognised because it is so pervasive.

The central thrust of O'Connell's political *praxis* was the organisation and drilling of large numbers of people, the central technique of modern popular politics. In the British Isles, he was a generation ahead of his time, and his approach was copied by Liberals and Conservatives alike only after 1850. In the case of O'Connell's continually relabelled organ-isations, the local areas were organised, with the help of "missioners" from head office: the representative from Dublin would meet the local leaders, including the local parish priest or curate, and

> ...the priest tells his guest the effective strength of the district, availing himself, in the detail, of the local information possessed by the parishioners, or the neighbouring clergy, who have assembled at [the priest's] house. It is then ascertained who will work; who will undertake the duty of Repeal Warden; who will collect the Repeal rent; and who will assume the charge of particular ploughlands, if in the country, or wards, if in a town. The obstacles are also canvassed; the hostility of Lord so-and-so, or of Captain----, his agent, who swears he will eject every tenant who gives sixpence to any of O'Connell's devices!...The problem is speedily solved. What need Lord A or Squire B know about the tenants' contributions?[6]

O'Connell was not a universal-suffrage democrat, but a believer in a wide, but still restricted, manhood suffrage. In being such, he was a radical in his time, although he has since been anachronistically rebuked for it, much as Periclean Athens is nowadays occasionally idiotically con-demned for its anti-feminism. Another very practical and, ironically, *democratic* reason for taking the vote away from the poor, as in the case of the Forty-Shilling Freeholders, was the fact that they were particularly vulnerable to intimidation by their landlords.

O'Connell's whiggism and his royalism, combined with the hostility of Young Ireland, meant that the intellectual tradition of Irish nationalism tended to write him out of the canon as it veered more towards separatist republicanism after 1848; by Pearse's time, secondary figures such as Emmet and Tone, and profoundly unattractive ones such as John Mitchel, had been built up in an attempt to overshadow O'Connell. In the strange and central figure of the de Valera of the 1926-75 era we see a synthesis; a figure whose insurrectionist and neo-Gaelic ideology hides a deep, if perhaps subconscious, understanding of the political techniques of O'Connell. The romantic visions of the Little Tradition are finally harnessed to the classical practicalities of the Great, in the form of the Fianna Fáil party. It is truly fortunate that such a cultural synthesis, however illogical it might appear to be, did occur in Irish political culture.

3

MAKING NATIONS: O'CONNELL, RELIGION AND THE CREATION OF POLITICAL IDENTITY

Brian Girvin

Daniel O'Connell's contemporary relevance is not at first apparent. His eighteenth-century world has been erased by the impact of the Famine, the Land League and the republican tradition. He seems a distant figure rather than one addressing the problems of the late twentieth century. In so far as he is remembered, it is on sentimental grounds rather than for his contribution to the solving of contemporary problems. His commitment to non-violence is sometimes cited in the context of the continuing war in Northern Ireland, but no workable solution has yet been adduced from his thought or actions which might be relevant to that conflict. However, the O'Connell contribution to the making of modern Ireland remains central, if somewhat ambiguous. He is rightly celebrated as the man who led the successful movement which secured Catholic Emancipation from a reluctant British government, but is often criticised for his refusal to condone violence when Repeal was refused. More generally his influence on the development of Irish nationalism is underestimated and greater emphasis is placed on the contribution of Wolfe Tone, the Fenians or Parnell to that ideology.

This conclusion is largely mistaken, so it is necessary to reassess O'Connell's contribution. He exercised a formative influence over the growth of a Catholic democracy in Ireland and particularly over the extent to which that democracy would be both Catholic and nationalist rather than Catholic and British or republican and liberal. O'Connell was not the only influence during the years after the Union, but his role became so central that by 1824 a critic, but former ally, could claim that: "You are now, pre-eminently, the head of the Irish Catholics."[1] Though O'Connell was not, in the Nietzschean sense, above history, his career was such that early biographers often wrote of him in Promethean terms. Most of these studies were fiercely partisan, but they do grasp the radical impact which he had made not only on his co-religionists, but on Irish Protestants, the British government and on European opinion generally. As early as 1830 the political landscape in Ireland had been transformed and for Irish Catholics the Union had failed, though the means of resolving the tensions between the state and the Catholic democracy remained unclear. The Repeal movement was but the first of a series of attempts to resolve this.

None of this was inevitable; other outcomes were possible. That a particular denouement occurred is a result of the behaviour of specific individuals achieving ascendancy and others failing to do so; at certain crucial junctures such success can exclude most other options and impose limits on both contemporary participants and on subsequent political development. Between 1800 and 1825 O'Connell played this role and by the latter date the direction had been set along lines which were to be maintained until the late twentieth century. The Veto controversy, at its most intense between 1808 and 1815, established O'Connell as the foremost representative of Catholic Ireland, but also allowed him the opportunity to impress upon a body politic his particular vision of political culture. It is rare for an individual to be placed in this unique position. In the recent past de Gaulle played this role, while Ian Paisley in Northern Ireland and the Ayatollah Khomeini in Iran are parallel examples of the same phenomenon. These individuals seized an opportunity and moulded the political culture by doing so. Such a view of the historical "agent" rejects the idea that individuals are passive instruments of their political environment.

With the eclipse of Marxism (and with it the faddish determinism that passed for historical analysis since the 1960s) it may now be possible to return to a conception of history which pays closer attention to the relationship between historical events and the influence on them of ideas, individuals and faith (faith here means religious belief, which I distinguish from secular ideology). This implies a theory of historical opportunity and constraint which is not determinist, and which recognises that limits exist to human action. The outcome for a particular period is consequently a result of the interaction between the individual and the concrete historical context which the actions of individuals affect to a greater or lesser degree.[2]

THE UNION AND CATHOLIC POLITICS

O'Connell's entry into politics was not propitious; his speech in opposition to the Act of Union on 13 January 1800 acquired significance retrospectively only because a mass nationalist movement developed, many of whose aims had been defined by O'Connell. As his most recent biographer readily admits, the speech had little if any significance at the time, or indeed for some time thereafter. However, to claim that "Ireland lay inert in the aftermath of the Union; even the Catholic question fell away once Pitt was forced out of office because of his promise to press it upon the united Parliament", is to accept that an Irish nation was in existence in 1800 and that it contained the components identified by O'Connell. The speech contained the hope that such a nation should exist, but in terms of politics operated in the realm of wishful thinking. This can be seen from the flourish of his statement:

> that if the alternative were offered him of union, or the re-enactment of the penal code in all its pristine horrors, he would prefer without hesitation the latter, as the lesser and more sufferable evil; that he would rather confide in the justice of his brethren the Protestants of Ireland, who have already liberated him, than lay his country at the feet of foreigners.[3]

One motive for O'Connell's speech may have been to gain acceptance by the Irish bar. Nor was this the first occasion on which his attitudes coincided with a section of Protestant opinion. On 3 January 1797 he had appealed to Hunting Cap for permission to join the Lawyers' Corps, complaining that he was the only young lawyer not doing so. In a subsequent letter he emphasised the potential loss to himself and other property owners if revolutionary principles prevailed:

> That invasion which if successful should have shook the foundations of all property, would have destroyed our profession root and branch. All that I have read, all that I have thought, all that I have combined was about to be rendered nugatory at once. It was little. But this little was my all.[4]

During 1798 O'Connell's status anxiety became even more evident as the pressure on Catholics increased. Even before the rebellions of that year he was concerned that the limited Catholic relief which had been secured might be endangered. Though this did not occur there is enough evidence to conclude that O'Connell was deeply worried about his position in society and that he was prepared to defend that position. However, it would not be safe to conclude from this that O'Connell's participation in the Catholic meeting in 1800 was one simply of self interest.[5]

There were at least two reasons for his participation: the first was the fear shared by his fellow barristers that the Union would deprive them of income and status; the other was an attempt to formulate a notion of national appeal which would include the Catholic and Protestant Irish against the English. While O'Connell did not possess a consistent nationalist ideology at this time, nevertheless the nuances in the anti-Union speech can be considered national in the sense that he is appealing to common identity and distancing those whom he considers to be within that identity from those without (i.e. the classic inclusion and exclusion juxtaposition of modern nationalism). This has echoes of Tone and the republicans, but can be more easily placed within the development of O'Connell's political thought between 1790 and 1800. This thinking reflected the transition from what has been described as "Rationalist 'patriotism'" to "national self consciousness". His speech is an expression of the rationalism of the later eighteenth century but included elements of self-conscious nationalism. The appeal to Protestant and Catholic was influenced by eighteenth-century patriotism, as was the belief that the Protestants would deal equitably with Catholics. There is furthermore an unreality about the speech as O'Connell was willing to perpetuate the existence of a parliament which the Protestant Ascendancy had used to keep the Catholics in subjection. O'Connell's comment in 1798 that "The odium against the Catholics is becoming every day more inveterate. The Chancellor [Fitzgibbon] seems hardly disposed to leave them the privileges which they enjoy at present", continued to have force for the majority of Catholics.[6] In 1803 Denys Scully expressed a startlingly different view of the Catholic attitude to the Union:

> You see that the Faction, whom you dread, have changed sides, and are become the most discontented party in the country; that they are become the most clamourous against the British connection, because it has clipped their monopoly; that they are incensed by the late Union, which has demolished not our Parliament (for we had no share in it), but their club house.[7]

O'Connell's confidence in Irish Protestants had some basis in fact between 1800 and 1810. There were many, though not a majority, of Anglicans who sympathised with the Catholic demand for civil rights. Others, notably the northern Presbyterians, had a long tradition of political radicalism and a commitment to civil liberty, combined with a deep suspicion of Catholicism as an enemy of that liberty. It was well within the bounds of possibility that a movement could have been created to pressurise the British administration to act sympathetically in these matters. The nature of Irish politics after the Union did not preclude this. It is in this sense that I believe O'Connell's subsequent speech against the Union in 1810 should be interpreted. It is an essentially secular proclamation which places Repeal at the centre of his objectives. There is also a strong appeal for the unity of all Irish people against the British. Not just the establishment, but the very idea of Britishness is rejected. O'Connell is here already emphasising the separateness of Ireland from Britain and encouraging a spirit of collective identity among the Irish. If Britain is the enemy then only through co-operation within Ireland could anything be achieved:

> The Protestant alone could not expect to liberate his country — the Roman Catholic alone could not do it — neither could the Presbyterian — but amalgamate the three in the Irishman, and the Union is repealed. Learn discretion from your enemies — they have crushed your country by fomenting religious discord — serve her by abandoning it for ever... I require no equivalent from you — whatever course you shall take, my mind is fixed — I trample under foot the Catholic claims, if they can interfere with the Repeal...[8]

O'Connell then repeats his commitment of 1800 to preferring the reintroduction of the Penal Laws rather than accept foreign rule. There can be little doubt that during this decade O'Connell formulated a view of nationalism which included all Irish people and excluded the British; Repeal follows naturally from that. His rhetorical device on the Penal Laws reflects a genuine belief that it was better to wait for reform from fellow Irishmen than to gain it from a foreign power. Yet it is still only his own view; one does not find the Catholic hierarchy, the aristocracy or the middle classes assenting to these views. Nor does one find it among the Protestant community outside of some republican groupings or the Orange faction whom O'Connell despised. There is a *prima facie* case to be made that even by 1810 a majority of Irish Protestants and a significant proportion of Irish Catholics continued to support the Union, or if the latter did not actively support it they did not see an alternative to it, certainly not the one which O'Connell was advocating.

The lack of response to O'Connell's appeal to Catholics not to sell their birthright in 1800 can be explained by the general belief that Pitt would introduce Emancipation in the near future and more generally to the absence of nationalism as we understand it today. The question of civil rights for Catholics was a demand for equality before the law and the full removal of all restrictions based on religion. Moreover, the agitation for such equality received support in many quarters at the end of the eighteenth century because in an age influenced by rationalism there appeared to be no good reason to deny it. Whatever O'Connell may have claimed there was little relationship between national identity and Emancipation at this stage of political development. Moreover, the British state was also rapidly changing and, while Catholic civil rights remained an issue which divided public opinion, there was a political constituency in Britain willing to offer a liberal solution to the outstanding difficulties. Irish Catholics may not have been overly enthusiastic about the Union, but as yet they were not, as a unified group, opposed to it.

Yet O'Connell's liberal appeal failed to mobilise Catholic, Protestant and Dissenter under the common name of Irishman. The secular republican alternative of Tone was even less successful. The attractiveness of British citizenship quickly lost its appeal for most Irish Catholics. Each of these appeals, in different ways, presumed an extraordinary sense of fluidity in terms of identity. Over the long run this fluidity was to prove illusory, yet for a brief moment a range of alternatives existed; not just in Ireland, but throughout Europe. The development of nationalism ended these possibilities while contributing to the maintenance of new and stronger rigidities in the form of national identity. These rigidities were new in form, though they drew on pre-nationalist forms of identity such as language, ethnic consciousness or religion. The moment of fluidity was brief, flourishing between 1780 and 1850. However, throughout this period it was impossible to predict the political environment which would emerge, the nature of the political culture in any given area or indeed the geographical extent of any state boundary. The French Revolution undermined the traditional sources of legitimacy and political order throughout Europe, permitting a level of unprecedented political experimentation. Discussing this impact on the state structure of Europe, Hobsbawm has concluded that:

> Between 1789 and 1815 few of them had not been transformed — even post-Napoleonic Switzerland was in important respects a new political entity. Such traditional guarantors of loyalty as dynastic legitimacy, divine ordination, historic right and continuity of rule, or religious cohesion, were severely weakened. Last, but not least, all these traditional legitimations of state authority were, since 1789, under permanent challenge.[9]

Experimentation operated at three levels. The established order had to adapt or be swept away; the United Kingdom and France offer contrasting examples. The new middle classes sought, and in some cases acquired, political power and the influence to reorder the management of the state or, increasingly frequently, developed a nationalist claim which challenged the existing state. Both the old and new elites attempted to gain legitimacy by appealing to the mass of the population, thus bringing about the democratisation of politics as a normal event.[10]

Ireland was not immune from these influences. The political ferment of the late eighteenth century and the first three decades after the Union attests to this. In these circumstances it was possible that a union could be effected between the diverse peoples on the island of Ireland, or between those of the two islands. That other outcomes occurred should not blind one to the possible alternatives. This was possible because during that time there was no heightened sense of national identity among the Irish political classes (i.e. those active in politics), whereas the development of such an identity created the conditions for the divisions which prevailed by the middle of the nineteenth century. Catholic, Protestant and Dissenter were strong sources of identity at the time, but in the face of rapid change each was being reassessed and reformulated, especially by the aristocratic, middle and artisan classes. These identities had yet to be linked to specific notions of national identity as distinct from those of community. In other words "making nations" also brings about other political responses which pre-national state formation or political organisation are usually free of. Because we live in an era dominated by political nationalism, there is an assumption that all political cultures are essentially nationalistic. What is often not recognised is the relative youth or modernity of nationalism itself. It might be urged that "ethnic" or religious identity is archaic, and that the process noted here is illusory; but what I am suggesting is that the continuity of such sources of identity does not preclude the transformation of them into something quite new in political terms.[11]

NATIONALITY AND RELIGION

If nationalism is a modern and novel phenomenon, as recent research into its origins has argued, then it is possible to detect the moment of its birth. If, as Benedict Anderson has claimed, nations are imagined communities, the constructs of middle class minds, it may also be possible to discover how this construct was erected (whether in the Irish or other cases).[12] Moreover, to say this is not to deny the legitimacy of nationalism as a source of political identity; it is to deny that nationalism is of ancient origin. But it is all the more important to identify the forces which brought it into being. We should recall that the revolutionary events of 1770-1820 transformed the entire landscape of Europe. A counter-revolutionary such as Joseph de Maistre recognised this when he sought to articulate a form of post-revolutionary conservatism.[13] The Industrial

19

Revolution in Britain, and the American and French political revolutions, challenged the existing elites and in most cases either replaced them or forced them to radically change their form of governing. More precisely most existing loyalties broke down (these include the formal authority structures central to the pre-revolutionary monarchies) and had to be reconstituted on a new basis (as was the case in Britain), or entirely new loyalties had to be generated. In the case of Britain "state based patriotism" was remarkably successful in sustaining legitimacy in a changing context, whereas in most other states or regions this did not suffice.[14]

Where this was not possible nationalism often provided the legitimacy for new loyalties, but because they were not based on the state they proved remarkably destructive. The transformation of nationalism as the primary form of identity has been most recently traced by Eric Hobsbawm who argues for the uniqueness and the relative modernity of such an outcome. Walter Bagehot and John Stuart Mill by mid-century had recognised that the political systems of Europe had been transformed by this new movement and date its origins to the very end of the eighteenth century.[15] Lecky at the end of the century, though in some doubt as to the future of nationalism, concluded that it had transformed the state system as well as the domestic politics of most European states. Lecky's main concern is with liberty and he approvingly cites the existence of religious toleration in the Anglo-Saxon states as a good example of the extension of such rights. However, he adds that if nationalism and religion are linked then liberty will be in danger:

> No attentive observer can have failed to notice how frequently it displays itself in a desire to unify the national type, and to expel all alien and uncongenial elements. Religion more than any other single influence perpetuates within a nation distinct types and consolidates distinct interests.

Though citing anti-semitism as the main expression of such irrationalism, Lecky adverts to the general possibility that nationality and religion if fused would not be conducive to social peace or progress.[16]

Although the equation is often resisted in both Britain and Ireland, the history of nationalism elsewhere in the world demonstrates the powerful inter-relationship between religion, ethnicity and the emergence of national identity. Ethnic, regional and religious consciousness are pre-national forms of identity and solidarity which "nation makers" have drawn on to create a new form of identity. Indeed these building blocks have become the classic avenue for national development in the twentieth century. If, in addition, nationalism is not a feature of modernity but a collective reaction to the individualism central to the Enlightenment, then the correlation between religion and nationalism may be even stronger. This is not to claim that new nationalisms which derive their emotional and mobilising power from antecedent religious affiliation are theocratic (as is the case with contemporary Iran), but that religion serves a function which facilitates the integration of individual believers into a collective consciousness. Religion may also serve this function because of the juxtaposition between believers and non-believers, the faithful and heretics and the saved and the damned. The tradition of religious superiority and intolerance fits well with the claims of nationalism. Hobsbawm identifies the features which fuse the distinct elements and make the outcome so powerful:

> ...it is far from clear whether separate religious identity, however powerful, is, taken by itself, similar to nationalism. The modern tendency is to assimilate the two, since we are no longer familiar with the model of the multi-corporate state, in which various religious communities coexist under a supreme authority as in some senses autonomous and self administering entities...[17]

In the Irish case I am suggesting that this fusion had not occurred in 1800, but was effectively in place by the 1830s. If O'Connell's assertion of a common Irish identity in 1810 was "imagined", how did an Irish national identity become real, though in a form quite different from that envisaged? O'Connell's own political activities contributed to this. In the process of groping for the means to mobilise opinion for his idea of national identity he fused the demand for civil rights for Catholics with the demand for Repeal. Not only this, all the early forms of political mobilisation with which O'Connell was associated were related to religious issues, so that when the campaign for Repeal had gained acceptance by the mass of the Catholic political classes it was closely identified with the objectives of Catholicism. Increasingly, the symbols of the new nationalism and its personnel were such as to alienate those with different religious and cultural backgrounds (in the case of Ireland, Protestants). This was done inadvertently; O'Connell's protestations that his politics were not sectarian can be taken seriously, yet he himself was quick to denounce Protestant concerns as sectarian and not sincerely held. In a quite fundamental sense O'Connell was a victim of events outside his direct control. He could mould and direct but not control the changes which were taking place within Ireland and in Europe at this time.

In Ireland the relationship between religion and national identity is very powerful. This was not always the case. By the middle of the eighteenth century the traditional Irish Catholic association with the Stuart Pretender had weakened.[18] Catholic politics had by and large become liberal in the sense that the new urban middle class and the remnants of the aristocracy believed that their rights would be recognised by sympathetic governments. John Keogh, for example, believed that in order to convince the Protestant Ascendancy that this was a safe course of action it was necessary to operate within the constitutional structure. Such a strategy involved dissociating the Catholic body from republicanism, the French Revolution or Defenderism. By 1800 the results were clear for this strategy; many of the laws against Catholics had been relaxed, abandoned or ignored (the entry of Catholics into Trinity College Dublin is one case in point). These reforms had naturally increased the sense of alienation among those who had benefited from them, particularly those who had not experienced the reforming process itself. Although not exclusively an inter-generational question, the older Catholic activists were more cautious than their younger co-religionists. John Keogh's moderation (or conservatism) is attested to by his actions when the Catholic Committee divided on the question of whether a petition should be sent to Parliament in 1807 and again in 1808. These divisions were also present sometime later in the discomfort caused to older Catholics by O'Connell's attack on the Attorney General during the Magee case in 1813.[19]

The new young Catholics were both self confident and resentful, believing that Emancipation was a right rather than a concession for which they should be grateful. This was the section which O'Connell mobilised after 1808 against the older Catholic leadership, the Protestant Ascendancy in Ireland and the British government. The identity shared by the majority of those mobilised was at first Catholic rather than nationalist. It was this group which had most vigorously rejected the republican-nationalist identity which the United Irishmen and Wolfe Tone had offered to all the Irish.[20]

More than any other politician in Ireland O'Connell was in a position to influence the contours of the new nation. If at first O'Connell sought to develop a national consciousness which would appeal to all who lived on the island, he soon discovered that such an appeal was limited. In religion he found a more potent appeal and while his early involvement in Catholic politics did not diminish his commitment to Repeal, he quickly discovered that the emotive appeal of Catholicism was far stronger than that of Repeal of the Union. It was the Veto controversy which made O'Connell a public figure, and identified him personally with the more militant wing of Catholic politics. Moreover, in a more limited fashion to that of the 1820s, O'Connell mobilised a mass movement to outmanoeuvre the tactics of the British administration, the Protestant Ascendancy and conservative Catholic opinion. But he did more than that; he succeeded in identifying religion with the future of the nation and almost certainly produced the conditions which allowed for the overlap between religion and people which has prevailed until the present. This may have been unintentional, but in one sense it was inevitable in that once Emancipation was not carried by Pitt it would become the focus for agitation among Catholics. What was not inevitable was the form it took. The demand for securities by the British administration and by many Protestant sympathisers was not unusual. What was unusual was the violent mass opposition to the proposal, as Bishop Milner discovered when he wrote arguing for acceptance of the veto over the appointment of bishops.[21]

THE VETO CONTROVERSY AND IRISH NATIONALISM

The Veto controversy had its origins in the growth of tolerance towards Catholics in Ireland and the impact of the French Revolution on the Papacy. The 1793 Relief Act, the establishment of Maynooth and the Union itself can be interpreted as part of a process by which the British government, often in the face of opposition by the Irish Protestant Ascendancy, attempted to reconcile Catholics to the Crown. Moreover, the French Revolution, by undermining the traditional cleavage based on religion, now forced both Catholics and Protestants to co-operate as conservatives against revolution and anti-clericalism. Both Protestant and Catholic rulers and Churches could find common cause against what was usually considered to be an anti-religious force.[22] One consequence of these developments was that the British government sought arrangements with the Irish hierarchy which would ensure the loyalty of the Irish Catholic population. These were forthcoming not only from the Church, but from the Catholic aristocracy and the middle classes.[23] The Bishop of Cork, Francis Moylan, in a pastoral in response to the 1798 Rebellion concurred with the opinion of the Archbishop of Dublin that all such acts were contrary to the Church's teaching. Most of the pastorals during the 1790s by members of the hierarchy were legitimist in tone and intent, seeking to reinforce what was believed to be true authority. Moylan also urged the Catholic population to recognise the benefits which Catholics had received from the British administration, in his opinion the most generous to date. He was subsequently to support the Union on these grounds, and endorsed a view that Lord Cornwallis was "the saviour of Ireland".[24]

It is in these circumstances that the hierarchy agreed to consider whether the government should be given some influence over the appointment of bishops by the Pope. In January 1799 ten bishops, meeting in Maynooth, agreed that some such arrangement would be acceptable under specified circumstances. The most important clause stated that:

> Should the government object to a named candidate, that objection to
> be lodged within one month after presentation to the president of the
> election who shall forthwith arrange for another election. [25]

These arrangements remained secret until 1808, but had been negotiated in
the belief that they would be a *quid pro quo* for Emancipation after the
Union. When they became public in 1808 circumstances had changed
considerably: Emancipation had not been conceded, Pitt had resigned over
the issue and subsequently felt unable to fulfil his commitments, while in
1807 the election was fought and won by the King's party on an essentially
"No Popery" platform.

That the veto was a trade-off in very difficult circumstances is evident
from the correspondence between members of the Irish hierarchy at the
time and from the position of the Catholic Church in revolutionary
Europe. There was considerable unease among the bishops concerning the
implications of the original decision. Despite this, the Church and
middle class opinion remained legitimist, supporting the government and
the Union. Denys Scully actively supported the Union, believing that
those aristocrats who had left Dublin after 1800 were not sympathetic to
Catholic demands. Indeed they "would involve all things in confusion and
ruin rather than consent to the Emancipation of the Catholics". Not only
do Catholics generally appear to have supported the Union, but they also
opposed republicanism in 1798 and again in 1803. A distinction should be
drawn between the bulk of Catholic property owners and the educated
classes who sought constitutional change, and the non-propertied who
were more open to sectarian and revolutionary influence.[26] Scully's own
pamphlet cited above was well received by both Catholics and Protestants and represented the opinions of an influential section of Catholics
at that time. According to Scully "A change of measures and of men had
taken place" since the Union:

> You see that it is the interest and principle of the present Government,
> who espouse no party, to treat all with impartiality and justice; that, if
> you continue cordially to support them, they in return, will continue to
> protect you and reward you with their esteem and confidence.[27]

The intent of this pamphlet was to demonstrate the essential liberalism
of the existing situation and the possibilities for future beneficial change.
It is a similar belief which underlines Archbishop Troy's circular letter of
May 1802 deploring Pitt's failure to introduce Emancipation, but commend-
ing Catholics to continued moderation: "The Catholic body will therefore
see how much their future hopes must depend upon strengthening their
cause by good conduct in the meantime." Critics, he argues, "may be
assured that Mr Pitt will do his utmost to establish their cause in the pub-

lic favour and prepare the way for their finally obtaining their objects".[28]

In so far as a determinable position can be attributed to the Irish Catholic polity prior to 1808, it is one which was constituted by a number of elements: loyalism, liberalism and "proto-nationalism".[29] As yet there is little evidence that the Catholic middle class had discarded loyalism (one observer claimed that O'Connell remained an "Orange Catholic" until 1810).[30] Catholic political objectives remained civil rights within the United Kingdom; only later did this demand come to be identified with separatism. Civil and economic disabilities do not necessarily promote separatism; in the case of British Non-Conformism it contributed to political radicalism and demands for reform of the relationship between a religious body and the state. That this was not forthcoming in the Irish case can be attributed to a number of factors: the actions of King George III in opposing Catholic reforms alienated many, the death of Pitt deprived the cause of a strong proponent, while the evidence of popular anti-Catholicism in Britain itself led many to doubt the efficacy of seeking reform within the United Kingdom. Emancipation was not at first an issue of national identity but one of recognising the civil rights of a minority of demonstrably loyal subjects by a Protestant state. Equality of citizenship was the key demand of the Catholic Committees in both England and Ireland, and was particularly well articulated by the Catholic aristocracy in each country. If Emancipation had been conceded prior to 1808 there was a strong possibility that the Catholic Irish would have become British in much the same way as the Protestant Irish (especially the northern section) did in the course of the nineteenth century.

When Henry Grattan announced in Parliament in 1808 that Catholic opinion was willing to accept a veto as part of the resolution to the outstanding restrictions on Catholics, his claim to represent either the Irish hierarchy or Catholic opinion in Ireland was quickly repudiated in what was a spontaneous rejection of his proposals. The conservative Archbishop Troy of Dublin, the member of the hierarchy probably closest to the British administration, reflected the change in mood over the decade in a quite self-conscious fashion:

> In the former we were called upon, pending the Union question, by an Administration supposedly friendly, and holding out the prospect, if not an implied promise, to consider the measure as the condition of Emancipation. At the present our hopes have not only been blasted, but a No Popery Administration declares in both Houses of Parliament that we are to expect nothing more.[31]

On 14 September the hierarchy passed two resolutions which in the popular mind represented a rejection of the veto. While Troy did not admit such a construction of the meeting, his own careful assessment of the events indicates that considerably more was at stake.[32] The mobilisation of Catholic opinion on a religious issue was neither unusual nor surprising. What was surprising was the link made between a religious issue and national identity. As Oliver MacDonagh has noted: "Although the issue at stake was, narrowly viewed, ecclesiastical, it also involved the Irish prelacy in the public espousal of a popular, liberal and nationalistic cause."[33]

It is quite different to the apostacy of Bishop Butler of Cork which could be interpreted as an isolated incident resulting from complicated circumstances, and which had little long-term ecclesiastical or political impact.[34] The controversy which followed the events of 1808 transformed not only the Irish hierarchy and Irish Catholic opinion, but it contributed to the divisions between Catholics and Protestants within Ireland which have prevailed since then. If the revolutionary events of 1789-1815 undermined loyalties which had to be remade, those events in Ireland unmade the slow incorporation of Irish Catholics into the British body politic, generated a heightened awareness of what it meant to be Catholic in a Protestant state, and provided a necessary element of combustible material for the emergence of Irish nationalism. Once the Irish Catholic community perceived itself as different, and believed or was persuaded that its condition was due to the actions (or inactions) of an alien administration or state, then the foundations for autonomous national development had been laid.[35] That this occurred in Ireland at this time should not be surprising if it is accepted that the political environment was open to influence in a number of directions. The country was poised between a number of alternatives, none of which had yet been realised in political terms. The impetus came from the veto itself, from the changing assumptions within the Catholic community and from the entry of O'Connell into the mainstream of Catholic and Irish politics. The veto did not create Irish nationalism, but it did provide a catalyst for mobilisation which permitted it to emerge.

The Veto controversy coincides with and prompts the eruption of the Catholic masses into Irish political life. Eschewing the revolutionary republicanism of the United Irishmen and Robert Emmet, the Catholic middle classes in particular are mobilised by the veto issue along lines which increasingly distinguish them from Irish Protestants and the British state. It was largely, though not exclusively, an urban phenomenon drawing in the relatively prosperous and educated. It also produced a considerable pamphlet literature which reflects the social nature of the conflict.[36] Although not as inclusive as the Catholic Association campaign at the end of the 1820s, the mobilisation remains a significant contribution to the democratisation of Irish politics because of the large numbers of Catholics participating in the debates. The controversy led to the marginalisation of the aristocracy and their middle class allies within Catholic politics even before they seceded from the Catholic Board in a fit of pique with O'Connell. Thomas Wyse described this section of Catholic politicians as those who "...crept ingloriously away from the contest, and allowed themselves to be trampled into obscurity by numbers".[37] From the outset the vetoists lost the political initiative. Following what was considered to be a condemnation of the 1808 proposals by the hierarchy an address of thanks to the bishops was signed by 40,000 people, whereas an address to Lord Fingall, the main advocate of the veto, was signed by fifty, forty-six of whom later retracted.[38] Similarly Bishop Milner, who was believed to have been the main architect of the proposals, was left in little doubt as to popular opinion when he visited Ireland and especially Cork in the autumn of 1808. Such was the popular hostility to him on the issue that he changed his mind and moved to the anti-vetoist camp soon thereafter.[39]

The difference between vetoists and anti-vetoists in 1808 may have been tactical. Archbishop Troy certainly believed that the hierarchy's resolutions in that year did not preclude some negotiated settlement along similar lines in the future. For some at least opposition to the veto was contingent and allowed for flexibility subsequently. However, as the issue re-emerged between then and 1815 on a number of occasions each side became more polarised. Irish opinion was outraged in 1810 when the English Catholic Board appeared to accept the veto in return for Emancipation. John Keogh, Scully and O'Connell were agreed on the need for opposition to the so-called "Fifth Resolution", although differing on many other issues. Furthermore, resolutions from a number of areas in Ireland deplored and condemned any proposals which sought to impose securities in return for Emancipation.[40] The Irish hierarchy unanimously adopted sixteen resolutions at a Synod in Dublin on 26 February 1810 which reinforced the 1808 resolutions, and explicitly endorsed the actions of the Catholic Committee, and O'Connell in particular, for their role in opposing the veto.[41] A resolution in support of the bishops was passed by the Irish laity on 2 March which reasserted what was becoming the received wisdom among them:

> ...as Irishmen and Catholics we never can consent to any dominion or control whatsoever over the appointment of our Prelates on the part of the Crown or the servants of the Crown.[42]

In public statements and in the pamphlet literature Irish and Catholic become interchangeable, and the independence of episcopal appointments is identified with national consciousness. However, these views were not universally shared by Irish Catholics. The aristocracy had considerable reservations, while some sections of middle-class Catholic opinion remained uneasy concerning the consequences of the agitation. Though it would be unreasonable to generalise on the issue, there were those who considered themselves to be Catholic Irish liberals, and who desired full citizenship within the British state. They were not unhappy with the prospect of state control over episcopal nomination, believing this to be more acceptable than nomination by the Pope. The poet Thomas Moore, in a rejoinder to the 2 March resolution, warned Catholics not to be revengeful for past wrongs, but to accept a veto in order to reconcile Catholics and Protestants to one another. He concluded that Protestant fears were not unfounded:

> The Protestants fear to entrust their constitution to you, as long as you continue under the influence of the Pope; and your reason for continuing under the influence of the Pope, is that you fear to entrust your Church to the Protestants. Now I have shown, I think, in the preceding pages, that *their* alarm is natural, just and well founded, while *yours* is unmeaning, groundless and ungenerous. It cannot, therefore, be doubted by which of you the point should be conceded.[43]

Though others argued in similar vein over the next decade, their arguments proved ineffectual and their influence limited.[44] Moore's pamphlet appears to have been aimed at O'Connell and Scully, but if so it did neither any political harm.[45] Indeed, O'Connell seized the opportunity to increase his influence within both the Catholic Committee and among the wider Catholic public as a direct result of the agitation in 1810.[46] His speech on the Union in 1810 is the last which asserts the primacy of Repeal over Catholic claims. Over the next five years O'Connell's political rhetoric becomes more decidedly Catholic to the extent that he gives that aim a priority over Repeal. Moreover, as he became more immersed in Catholic politics the tendency grew to identify Catholic and Irish. This is part of a wider issue of identity. Isaiah Berlin has suggested that there is a strong need among humans to identify with those similar to oneself in language, race, culture or religion. The transformation of Islam over the past two decades may offer a clue to O'Connell's behaviour. It is now common to find the Western-educated elite in Islamic states embracing at the very least the form, but frequently also the substance, of the faith following a period of seduction by the secular West. O'Connell may be a very early example of the successful attraction of tradition over modernity.[47]

At a more personal level it is also important to recognise that O'Connell's activities on the veto issue paralleled his own identification with the spirit and forms of the Church. A Deist when young and a Freemason for much longer, he became increasingly pious and strict in the observance of his religious duties. In 1809 Mary O'Connell is urging him to fast during Easter Week, perhaps recognising that his return to the Church may not have been complete: "And Good Friday the *judges* will go to prayers and certainly you can then *spare time* to go. At all events I hope you will hear prayers on Easter Sunday." By 1816 she is remonstrating with him for being too strict in his observance. It is difficult to detect from his correspondence the depth of this commitment, but it was certainly genuine. The question remains open as to the extent to which this change affected his political thinking and actions. My own suspicion is that it is no coincidence that O'Connell identified not only with the Catholic people but with its ritual at a time when he was constructing a mass political movement around religious issues.[48]

When Henry Grattan introduced his Emancipation bill in 1813, it originally contained no securities or veto. However, it is probable that the bill in this form was not intended as the final statement, but as a basis for negotiating a settlement to the Catholics' outstanding claims. In any event, Grattan did not oppose the amendments proposed by George Canning which maintained the need for government control over clerical appointments. Canning had been one of the leading Tory supporters of Emancipation, but believed that a veto was necessary both on grounds of political expediency and on principle. In this Grattan and liberal opinion generally concurred.[49] A number of factors contributed to the belief that a veto was required if Emancipation was to be conceded. Most influential Protestants continued to be suspicious of Catholicism as a superstitious and disloyal religion, the believers in which owed allegiance to an external authority. However, this suspicion had been attenuated somewhat by the impact of the French Revolution on all religions. Liberal Protestants believed that religious freedom should be recognised in an age of tolerance. However, this was often accompanied by the belief that Catholicism would become "Protestant"; that Catholics would continue to believe in the ritual and dogma of Catholicism, but would not owe allegiance to the Pope. Henry Parnell, one of the leading advocates of Emancipation, continuously reminded Irish Catholic leaders that Protestants had a real fear of the Papacy.[50] Moore had adverted to this fear in 1810, though there is little evidence that the Irish Catholic polity accepted such distinctions during 1813. Yet the Papacy had undergone a revival during the previous decade. Apparently decapitated by the French Revolution, it was merely stunned; the Concordat between Pope Pius VII and Napoleon in 1801 enhanced papal power in France, and was followed by the even more advantageous Italian Concordat in 1803. The revival of papal influence, though still restricted by Napoleon, worried liberal Protestants. Events in Spain during the Peninsular War may also have contributed to Protestant doubts that Catholicism was in any way moderate or tolerant, a concern further reinforced by the behaviour of the Church and Catholic monarchs after the 1815 Restoration.[51]

Richard Lalor Sheil, the Catholic playwright and politician, warned O'Connell at the time that his actions in mobilising mass opinion against Grattan's bill were postponing Emancipation indefinitely. Although Sheil was later to become one of O'Connell's close allies, at this time they disagreed fundamentally about the veto. Sheil's fears were justified; the militant wing of the Irish Catholic Board strongly opposed the measure, as did Bishop Milner. In addition, the Irish hierarchy remained united in opposition to any legislation which contained a veto. Many English believed that this opposition swung parliamentary opinion against the bill. However, Sheil may have been overly optimistic. Emancipation was becoming more acceptable to British opinion, but this did not guarantee that a bill would be passed.[52] The outcome for Irish politics of this attempt at Emancipation was radical. A series of events, including the Magee case, the opposition to Grattan's bill, and the so-called "witchery" resolutions alienated aristocratic Catholic opinion. From 1813 the militant wing of Irish Catholicism was in the ascendancy with O'Connell as its representative figure. In the Catholic Board, where representation was socially narrow, O'Connell's majorities may not always have been secure, though increasingly they were; at the aggregate meetings, however, the popular mood was decidedly pro-O'Connell and anti-veto.

Nor was this confined to Dublin. At a meeting in Cork on 30 August 1813 O'Connell was chaired through the city after routing the aristocratic and merchant elite which had dominated the Catholic Board there. He informed his wife "...of the complete triumph which the people have had over the rascally Board who are now busy protesting and doing all the mischief that they possibly can. It is well, however, that their means of doing that mischief is now very limited indeed."[53] The incident in Cork reflects well the extent to which popular and Catholic politics had become intertwined. When a local landowner John Galway was nominated to chair the meeting, he was opposed by the crowd on the grounds that he had refused to support the resolution in favour of the bishops' stand on the veto. According to the reports he was forced to publicly repent for this action, prior to which the crowd had chanted: "We forgive them [vetoists] and may heaven forgive them." The outcome of the meeting was that a vote of thanks to Milner, Magee and O'Connell was carried by 10,000 to four. The figures may be exaggerated, but they reflect the advent of mass democratic politics in Cork and the ability of O'Connell to organise them. The large property owners then seceded and issued a statement opposed to the decisions taken. At a subsequent meeting this group asserted its superiority over the masses while continuing to advocate a veto:

> That adopting the wise principle of the constitution, by which property
> is made the standard of opinion, we found it impossible, at the late
> aggregate meeting, amidst the tumult of the lowest populace —
> ignorant of necessity, and misled by design — to ascertain the sense
> of the Catholics of this city and county.[54]

Later in the same year Catholic opinion was further divided by a
speech to the Catholic Board on 8 December by Dr Dromgoole during
which he criticised Grattan as a Protestant and the Protestant religion
itself. The result was an outcry by Protestant opinion and some liberal
Catholics. This led in turn to another meeting which condemned
Dromgoole and his sentiments as unrepresentative of Catholic opinion.
The decision dismayed much of Catholic opinion, and a further meeting
was called early in 1814 to reconsider the original condemnation. In the
event it was not rescinded and Dromgoole left Ireland for exile in Rome.[55]
The proposal to rescind the condemnation was moved by Aeneas McDonnell, editor of the *Cork Mercantile Chronicle*, who argued that attempts
to conciliate Protestants by condemning Catholics were of little value.
Denys Scully supported the motion to rescind and compared the attack on
Dromgoole to the persecution of Titus Oates. O'Connell, supporting Scully
and McDonnell, regretted the original censure vote, his own part in it and
"acknowledged his error" on that occasion:

> He condemned the conduct of the Board for the slavish feeling which
> would urge them to condemn a Catholic while they listened with
> forbearance to torrents of bigotry and calumnies...but the moment a
> Catholic dared to retort the calumnies of his slanderers, the Catholics
> raised their hands to break with their chains the head of their fellow
> slave.[56]

Although a minor incident in itself the Dromgoole case, if taken in the
context of other events in 1813, demonstrates the extent to which Catholic
politics had changed since 1803 when Scully had written his pro-Union
pamphlet. Irish identity was becoming increasingly associated with
Catholicism to the exclusion of Irish Protestants; it was also moving
towards separatism from the state. Moreover, the emergence of a mass
democracy largely mobilised on a religious issue secured this relationship.
Thus when the Quarantotti Rescript became known in Ireland in 1814 it
was almost universally rejected by clergy and laity alike, so that Protestant opinion was further alienated. These difficulties were reinforced
when the Pope in 1815 accepted a veto on appointments despite appeals
from Ireland.[57] However, by 1815 there was little support in Catholic
Ireland for accepting such a view even from the Pope. The issue was now
between a united Catholic Irish body and foreign influence whether papal
or British. Both in 1814 and 1815 the hierarchy declared against the

views promulgated in Rome, and in doing so broke decisively with its legitimist traditions and with the restorationist politics of the Papacy subsequently. After a meeting of the bishops on 23 and 24 August 1815 the hierarchy declared its opposition to the veto "...at all times and under all circumstances". The statement continued:

> ...we should consider ourselves as betraying the dearest interests of that portion of the Church which the Holy Ghost has confided to our care did we not declare most unequivocally that we will at all times and under all circumstances deprecate and oppose in every canonical way every such interference.[58]

This was a unanimous view, one now shared by even the most conservative of the bishops. Indeed, Bishop Moylan of Cork, frequently the butt of anti-vetoist criticism, expressed his condemnation of the Rescript shortly before his death in terms which O'Connell could have easily shared.[59] O'Connell himself warned Parnell in 1815 that the Catholic population would not accept a veto under any conditions and that any priest associated with it would lose his influence over the people.[60]

CONCLUSION

The veto question fizzled out shortly after 1815, but in the interim Irish politics had been transformed. O'Connell had created the first mass representative movement of the Catholic middle class and in so doing he had undermined the influence of the Catholic aristocracy and forced the Catholic Church in Ireland to choose between the nation and papal discipline. What is most remarkable is that O'Connell was able to forge such a movement on the basis of what at first sight was a fairly narrow point of religious principle. That it could generate such controversy demonstrates the shift in political consciousness which had taken place within a relatively short period, in particular the shift in loyalties which the emergence of a strong sense of Catholic identity had occasioned. The agitation also divided the anti-vetoists and, in the longer term, the entire Catholic population from their Protestant supporters in Parliament, many of whom feared what they believed to be the Pope's undue influence on the Irish Church. Grattan and Parnell, among others, were in favour of some type of qualified veto on the grounds that this would allay British Protestant fears and neutralise the "No Popery" sentiment then prevalent.[61] By 1815 O'Connell had secured the militant position on the veto, but by doing so had conflated Catholic and Irish to an extent not previously present.

In doing so he had harnessed the Catholic middle class to a sense of national identity deeply imbued with religious traits. The new Catholic polity was viewed with apprehension by Irish Protestants. This was reinforced subsequently by the campaign for Emancipation and later still during the campaign against tithes. On each occasion the object of mobilisation had a religious content, which in turn highlighted sectarian tensions in both parts of Ireland. The political outcome is clear. When O'Connell founded the Repeal movement, the Protestant community offered very little support for separatism. By the 1840s, consequently, the divisions within Ireland as well as those between Catholic Ireland and the British state had become firm.[62]

At the level of practical politics the Veto controversy is of little significance in comparison with Emancipation or Repeal. Its significance is as a point of departure in the fusing of religion and nationalism in Ireland. The consequences were far-reaching: it ended any possibility of a secular republican nationalism for all Irishmen; and it provided an emotional basis for national identity, but in doing so condemned Irish nationalism to reflect the values of a single denomination. The strength of feeling on the issue can be detected from the reaction to O'Connell's apparent compromise in 1825 on the issue of securities in return for Emancipation. His earlier speeches were cited against him, and only his popularity and the failure of the compromise itself saved him from the possibility of long-term odium.[63] While this may have been unwitting, O'Connell does appear to have perceived its nature. In a letter written to Bishop Doyle at the end of 1827 he identifies the nature of the new political force in Ireland as: "The combination of national action — all Catholic Ireland acting as one man — must necessarily have a powerful effect on the minds of the ministry and of the entire British nation."[64] At the end of his life the distinction between politics and religion becomes more blurred, whether during the controversy with Thomas Davis or in his private correspondence with Paul Cullen.[65]

Was this outcome inevitable? The foundations for a secular republican identity were extremely weak. It is doubtful if Protestant opinion anywhere in Ireland conceived of itself as Irish in the sense outlined by Tone or O'Connell. Irishness in either sense seems to have had a greater influence over Catholics than Protestants. Indeed in reaction to the national claims promoted by O'Connell and his successors, Protestants, more especially Northern Presbyterians, generated their own popular identity which was associated closely with anti-Catholicism. Identity in both parts of Ireland came to be refracted through religion. Association with a common British identity also proved impossible. This is in part attributable to the way in which Irish nationalism emerged at this time, but the anti-Irish (and anti-Catholic) nature of British popular culture is largely responsible. An element of elite culture desired compromise with

Ireland, but even that elite was divided on the terms, preventing a more open and generous approach to the problem.

Does this mean that sectarian politics were inevitable in Ireland? Not necessarily; there are examples in Europe where Catholics and Protestants, or Liberals and Catholics, have resolved their differences within a constitutional system acceptable to both sides. The Dutch system of *verzuiling* (pillarisation) stabilised conflict between contending, and apparently incompatible, traditions. The Belgian experience has even greater similarities with that of Ireland. A Catholic minority within a Protestant state, but with a strong liberal-secularist influence, established an independent state which recognised both the Catholic and liberal aspects of the community. A balance between the two was achieved which created a long-term consensus for political development. The Swiss cantonal system may also be appropriate to the resolution of conflict in this context.

None of these resolutions has proved attractive in Ireland. Liberalism has proved to be a very weak plant in these conditions, surviving in rare hothouse environments for most of the last two centuries. The type of liberal politics promoted by O'Connell, Bishop Doyle and others was not a contributory factor in the evolution of Irish nationalism during the second half of the nineteenth century. Although I do not wish to pursue this question at length here, I would suggest that liberalism in Ireland proved incompatible with democratic politics which, even among middle class Catholics and Protestants, remained essentially sectarian. This marks the limits of liberalism as a political philosophy; it may have been possible to be liberal in thought or writing, but this liberalism never penetrated the collective consciousness of the masses. Because O'Connell and others drew on Catholicism to provide substance for the movement for reform, they brought into play the "archaic" antagonism between Catholicism and Protestantism. For all his personal prestige O'Connell did not leave a legacy of Liberal Catholicism to Ireland. Having said that, O'Connell's contribution to Irish nationalism should not be underrated. He gave it the specific form which has lasted to the present. He made a major contribution to the modernisation of Irish political life, giving to the Catholic masses a strong sense of identity and meaning. One of the unintended consequences of this, however, was that in doing so they embraced an exclusive set of values which proved unattractive to the non-Catholic population of Ireland. There had been divisions between Catholic and Protestant prior to 1800, but the blending of religion and nationalism generated a political tradition which has often proved to be divisive subsequently.

4

LIBERTY AND CATHOLIC
POLITICS 1790-1990*

Fergus O'Ferrall

Political ideas associated with liberty are central to modern history. They are very pertinent in contemporary Ireland. It therefore seems important to explore such ideas in Irish Catholic politics since 1790. There is a too ready ascription of historical ideas on liberty to Protestant politics and this readiness is true of both Catholic and Protestant commentators. Indeed, many have argued and believed that Catholicism is essentially incompatible with liberalism. I wish to draw attention to the neglected Irish Catholic lineage of liberal politics. This lineage has significance not only in Ireland but also in a European and world context.

It is important to define the key terms: "liberty", "liberal", and "liberalism". I use them in the following way: "liberty" in the context of political history is concerned with extending the liberties or rights of the subject or citizen under constitutional rule; "liberal" is a label for those who wished to extend the liberties or rights of the subject or citizen, that is, those who advocated democratic reform and individual liberty; "liberalism" refers to the ideology of those who sought to establish a constitutional order with conditions "befitting a free man".

Liberty, liberal and liberalism carry a wide range of both positive and

---

* This article has been published in 1991 by the Freehold Press, Belfast.

negative associations in contemporary thought and discourse. There are core values which undoubtedly are "liberal" values — the central one being the prime valuation placed upon facilitating the fullest development and expression of the human personality. Furthermore, the word "liberal" carries connotations of "generous", "open-handed", "abundant" — important imaginative associations especially in Irish politics. The liberal vision is one of a general enlargement and freedom for the personality to flourish and of a rational direction of human life in society. Such a vision and set of values informed important Catholic literary and political figures in Irish history and provide a contemporary challenge for Catholic culture. It is not surprising that it is often through literature that we are equipped to imagine human variety and possibility. Literature is the human activity that takes fullest and most precise account of variety, possibility, complexity and difficulty in social relationships. Such imagining is essential to liberalism. Such a liberal imagination, I believe, has most to offer Catholics, Protestants and Dissenters, if they wish to share a common future on this island. It is vital to return to literature and seek out the roots of contemporary ideas on liberty; in this way we find inspiration from those who in their time espoused liberty and can now provide us with the imaginative reach, and sometimes the very language, with which to articulate our aspirations.

Lest this be thought a peculiarly unhistorical approach to the past, I begin the essay with a section on imagination and the past. This indicates that we inevitably select from the past using our contemporary concerns. I am suggesting that an imaginative concern for liberty ought to inform our exploration of the past, given the power of history over contemporary developments. The history which is influential on current events is always a "story-history" — a history which recounts, and makes contemporary, root experiences in our story of the past as a means of charting our way forward and informing our identity. To learn from history so that we can choose from the range of possibilities presented by the future requires a new dialogue between past and present. To ask the past new questions concerning "liberty" would result in a powerful new story on this island.

IMAGINATION AND THE PAST

History proper is the history of thought.
There are no mere events in history.

Seán O Faoláin prefaced his classic and exceptional book, *The Irish*, first published in 1947 (revised editions 1969, 1980) with this highly significant epigraph by R.G. Collingwood. It is the case that what we think about history is more important than the particular "facts" of history. Any understanding of Ireland's past is a combination of a "general theory" and of particular "facts" whether this "general theory" is consciously held, or simply an unconscious set of presuppositions. It is a vital and healthy exercise to spell out deliberately the theoretical framework adopted in any historical account. There is no escape into any "pure" history. Indeed whether history is experienced as an oppressive force or becomes a resource for human liberation depends upon how conscious we become of our "general theories" about the past. It also depends upon the quality of our historical imaginations.

A seminal illustration of the liberating potential of remembering the past is contained in the history of Israel as recorded in the Hebrew Bible. Here was a tiny people, "the least of all the peoples", on the fringes of the great empires over two millennia who were subjected to oppression, exile and ruin. Yet their story as presented in the Bible is the greatest attempt yet made to wrestle with destiny, interpret history and discover meaning in human drama. Ultimately, this is because of the way they *imagined* their past: the root relationship in their history is that of the individual personality within the community in covenant with Yahweh or the Divine Personality. The value of studying the ancient story of the Hebrews, with their unique historiography, rests on the fact that their finer spirits discerned the hand of God in past events.

What was unique about the Israelites was their interpretation of history — that God was active in history and Lord of history, and that it was important to identify and keep remembering, re-enacting, or re-interpreting certain key episodes, like the Exodus, to sustain the people even through catastrophes such as the Babylonian Exile. What is striking is this creative use of the past (selectively and sometimes even inaccurately recorded) to envision a purpose, a present and a future for a people no matter how grim the circumstances.

There is a paradigm here in approaching history as the updating or contemporising of tradition. Essentially, all history is "story-history" in that it is not a detached report of events; neither is it simply a tale spun out of the imagination. "Story-history" is about retrieving, and making contemporary, root experiences in the past.

A quotation from Saint Augustine helps to highlight the fact that we *are* sovereign over time, yet we often fail to recognise the static conceptual power of terms like "past", "present" and "future":

> ...it is abundantly clear that neither the future nor the past exist, and therefore it is not strictly correct to say that there are three times, past, present, and future. It might be correct to say that there are three times, a present of past things, a present of present things, and a present of future things. Some such different times do exist in the

mind, but nowhere else that I can see. The present of past things is the
memory; the present of present things is direct perception; and the
present of future things is expectation.[1]

In respect of the past we can only know "a present of past things";
therefore we must take responsibility for our conscious *use* of the past in
the light of our present perceptions. The alternative is to believe in a
myth of "objective" history and this is to give unnecessary power to "the
past" so that it dominates and oppresses us.

For Irish people, no less than for the Hebrews of old, the imaginative
exploration of our memories is perhaps our greatest resource in coming to a
renewed awareness of identity and in the formation of our personalities.
One liberation theologian speaks of such a process as "to rememorate", to
make the past present and effective, to re-read and re-live the past, to
appropriate significant events in the light of what is important for the
contemporary situation. "To remember" in the Bible is to participate
again in a liberating event. This is a vital imaginative notion because "to
remember" for Irish people generally has meant "to imprison". The recur-
ring and imprisoning cyclical pattern of the Irish nationalist historical
memory is neatly encapsulated in the 1916 Proclamation and enshrined in
the Preamble to the 1937 Constitution. This pattern reduces the historical
experience of "the Irish people" to a linked series of militant uprisings
over "seven hundred years" of British oppression. It is fundamentally and
profoundly *reactionary* in its commitment to an idealised and unchanging
relationship with Britain. A key question, therefore, concerns the role
memory plays in keeping us victims of our past and the possible role it has
in equipping us to be inheritors of our future.

There exists a universal desire to make sense of history by making a
"story" or by telling "stories". By creatively re-interpreting the past such
narratives can serve to retrieve new and hitherto concealed possibilities
in our past. I want to contest the idea that there exists an objective record
of the past scientifically established by professional historians. Sometimes Leopold Von Ranke's famous words *wie es eigentlich gewesen* are
paraphrased as "what actually happened" when a more accurate translation is surely "what truly is", what truly existed. Truth, as the Israelite
historians recognised, is a many-faceted jewel when relating past
developments to present needs. Certainly, there are recognised skills and
proven methods for historians which add immensely to our knowledge of
what happened in the past but the key is always the "general theory" or
"theories" with which this knowledge is apprehended. The historian's
job is to identify the thought behind each past act, and also to measure
the thought's worth or worthlessness. As Joseph Lee has so ably reminded
us, our intellectual processes, and their quality, are crucial. Eminent

historians, for example, in the 1920s and 1930s, according to Lee, produced "vintage cowboy and indian stuff" and until recently, despite the high quality of historical writing, Irish historians were very reluctant to confront the contemporary or even the twentieth century. Unlike the historians of ancient Israel, Irish historians have failed to make the contribution which is so necessary to contemporary Irish society by furnishing our political imaginations with relevant "root experiences".

Irish historiography, since the 1930s, has been devoted to a particular concept of history: history as "essentially the study of institutions, mainly political and ecclesiastical, rather than of society or of mentalities". There remain, as Lee says, vast tracts of Irish spiritual, intellectual, cultural and material experience to be explored. Irish history, in Lee's words, "proved unable to encompass within its conventional categories the range of relationships crucial to understanding the functioning of contemporary Irish society".[2]

Two things therefore are critical in approaching our history — firstly, the general "theory" or body of ideas we bring to the task and, secondly, the fact that the contemporary needs which we feel or identify are legitimate determinants of what we select from our past experiences as significant for us.

THE LIBERAL TEMPER

I am suggesting that these things be recognised and that we accept that historians, in any event, despite claims of objective and scientific methods, have *always* allowed their current dispositions to influence their choice of topics, themes and "facts" from the past. Let us make these things explicit and, as far as possible, let us identify our contemporary concerns when looking at our past in such a way as to make a genuine contribution to a fresh dialogue between past and present. Ideas associated with liberty are, it seems to me, the most pertinent to contemporary Irish society after decades of violence and suffering and they provide a most appropriate prism through which we might view our historical experiences.

My explicit argument is that the liberal mind and imagination have most to offer Catholics, Protestants and Dissenters if they are to share a common future on this island. I should like to introduce it with a quotation from an American historian, Gordon Wright:

> In an age of unprecedented complexity, when ideological fanaticism, sporadic bursts of tribal fury, and the advocacy of "realism" in both its crude and its sophisticated form put world stability and even human existence at risk, the liberal temper may offer the nearest thing to a

set of guideposts through the mine field. Its rejection of a black-and-white world in which the battalions of good and evil line up in serried ranks; its awareness of ambiguity as a profound and pervasive presence in human affairs; its respect for such qualities as scepticism, tolerance, fair-mindedness, and what George Orwell called (for want of a more precise term) "decency" — these traits combine to make up a world view that in some ways overlaps those of the radical or the conservative, but that possesses its own integrity, its central core of values by which to judge the past and to relate that past to the present.[3]

The "liberal temper" does, I believe, offer most in selecting "guideposts" through the mine field of modern Irish history.

LIBERAL SIGNPOSTS 1790-1990

Ó Faoláin's pioneering study of the Irish mind, *The Irish*, which he significantly termed "a creative history", employs in one place the image of the "signpost" when speaking of an historical event which points forward to a modern development. It is an instructive exercise to attempt to identify personalities or events in Irish history which point forward to greater human liberty. I will select a few signposts from Irish Catholic politics since the time of the French Revolution highlighting issues which still trouble the competing groups on this island. History does indeed contain "encouraging signposts as well as depressing culs-de-sac", to use Roy Foster's phrase.[4]

The early 1790s marks the rise of representative leadership within the Irish Catholic community, with the election of a new Catholic Committee in 1790, to be followed by the holding of the Catholic Convention in December 1792, which has been described as "probably the most representative group that had ever gathered in Ireland".[5] Our period ends in 1990 with an Irish government holding the Presidency of the European Community at the start of another critical decade in European affairs.

In these two hundred years, and between these two highly symbolic and important occasions, occurred an epic struggle by Irish Catholics comparable to, though not on the same scale of human suffering as, the modern folk trauma of the Jewish people. Central to this struggle, if not always explicitly stated, was the effective Irish question which burdened the Catholic mind: how to adapt to the modern world without ceasing to be Catholic and/or Irish?

It has been through representative institutions that this question has been debated and partially answered. Those who espoused violence most often were, in effect, *reactionaries* to the modern world, having renounced the option of accommodating to it.

40

The ideology of violence in modern Irish politics has its roots in the agrarian secret societies. As Oliver MacDonagh has noted, "much of the agrarian violence which bred or supported political conspiracy was, literally speaking, reactionary in aim." The ideology embraced Tone's dogma that reaction against the British connection — "the unfailing source of Ireland's ills" — was central. As Liam de Paor has pointed out, the republican tradition quite early in the nineteenth century "under the powerful influence of romantic nationalism, was diverted on to a switchline: liberty became a matter not so much for individuals as for *nations*, to which individuals were subordinated." This involved cultural separatism and the reaction against the "modern world" found, for example, in the Young Irelanders.

This reactionary Irish ideology of violence was rounded out by the Fenians and Pearse: from Fenianism came the assertion that Ireland was in a constant state of war with Britain, as well as the assumption of governmental rights by a militant conspiracy; from Pearse came the "religion" of violent nationalism, the cults of blood, youth and sacrifice and the concepts of generational witness, historic roles and the supremacy of the gesture.

This is the historic background to Irish proponents of violence and to their use of the past and it has resulted in self-selected groups assuming for themselves an *élite* role in Irish affairs. As de Paor says, they are "ultimately anarchic, self-obsessed and self-sufficient, dedicated not so much to an imagined future as to an imagined past."[6]

The "signposts" we seek, however, in respect of individual liberty are to be found in the roots and growth of Irish representative or democratic political mechanisms. They mark the turning points in the persistent Irish parliamentary tradition. These "signposts" help us to understand the contemporary adherence by the great majority of Irish Catholics to constitutional liberties through free institutions.

As Brian Farrell wrote in 1973, it was "through parliament and largely within parliament that Ireland grew to both nationhood and independence". As Farrell recognised, this parliamentary thread

> ...is a much more complex, confused and insecure guide than the single searing torch with which Pearse sought to illuminate all aspects of the Irish historical maze. It offers no simple certainties and proffers few unquestioned dogmas. The Irish parliamentary tradition is not marked by any steady and unbroken progress towards greater freedom and greater participation in government but stumbles on by a series of doubtful fits and uncertain starts. Its major actors have not been legendary heroes and villains cast in an epic mould, but everyday men of affairs — creatures, like the rest of us, in whom there is room for good and ill, for calculating self-interest and for nationwide largeness of heart; men in whom the petty and the proud, the

mean and the magnificent, the narrow bounds of practical realities
and the wider horizons of great political visions were mixed.[7]

I believe it is crucial "to rememorate" the "story" (or "stories") of this
liberal democratic past. We have in our political culture been extraordinarily reluctant to cherish or tell this "story" — yet it is arguably the
most important "story" we have to tell the world. How and why did the
Catholic Irish who were totally outside the province of politics, law and
government in the eighteenth century come to be *the* pioneers, in the world
colonial context, of democratic politics, of the modern political party, free
elections, democratic opposition and political liberty in the nineteenth
and twentieth centuries?

Irish Catholics from the 1790s had to be creative in politics or remain
outside of politics. Two major responses were evolved in terms of values
and cultural traditions. The first may be termed the "Irish-Enlightenment" response and the second the "Gaelic-Romantic" response.[8] The first
may be generally characterised as modern, cosmopolitan, secular and
democratic whereas the second was traditional, local, rural, Catholic,
anti-British, prone to violence. Of course, these responses sometimes
merged and reinforced each other and sometimes they conflicted even to
the extent of civil war, as in 1922 or since 1969 in Northern Ireland.

The Enlightenment tradition assumes the separation of religion from
the political process. The notion of a *religious* attachment as justifying a
political claim is inherently repugnant to what has been the dominant
intellectual tradition in the West. The rhetoric of the three great
Western revolutions inspired by the Enlightenment — the English,
American and French revolutions — had predominated in international
political discourse. This rhetoric, based on Enlightenment values — the
rule of law, freedom of expression and political democracy — is in sharp
contrast to the values of traditional societies such as that inhabited by
most of the Catholic Irish as they entered the modern world. Those who
speak for the people of traditional societies may assume Enlightenment
rhetoric for wider consumption, masking non-Enlightenment aspirations.
The classic modern example of this is the conflict between Jew and Arab in
the Middle East.[9] The course of political development in Ireland from the
1790s to the 1990s offers an extended example of this clash of Enlightenment with "tradition", and careful attention to what politicians *do* as
well as to their rhetoric is advisable.

The Catholic Convention of 1792 was the first of a long line of alternative representative institutions created by Catholic leaders. It is
significant that the "parliamentary" forum was created on the assumption that political change could be effected through adapting British
constitutional laws and principles. This was the hope which inspired the

first half of the 1790s and which became central to Daniel O'Connell's long political career in the first half of the nineteenth century.

O'Connell was, in large measure, the product of the radical political thought which he absorbed in the 1790s. He was particularly attracted to William Godwin's *Political Justice*. Oliver MacDonagh has written in his recent biography:

> Where Godwin really struck home with O'Connell was, first, in his total opposition to violence and revolution as bound to hold back the long march of rational progress...and secondly, his conviction that the key to every beneficial change lay in the enlistment of public opinion...O'Connell's entire political structure was to rest, ultimately speaking, on these two simple propositions.[10]

O'Connell was, indeed, one of the great carriers, as MacDonagh has noted, of the historic liberal tradition of the Enlightenment and the *philosophes*.[11] If we wish to get to the heart of the Irish democratic and liberal tradition we must begin with O'Connell. He displayed total commitment to political equality, to humanitarian reform, to anti-imperalist and anti-racialist politics. O'Connell, uniquely among Catholic statesmen of his period, espoused the complete separation of church and state and he struggled to establish religious liberty upon a general principle which would give religious freedom to all, whether Jew, Muslim, Christian, Catholic or Protestant:

> My political creed is short and simple. It consists in believing that all men are entitled as of right and justice to religious and civil liberty.[12]

It is not being claimed here that O'Connell's politics was divorced from Gaelic and traditional society — on the contrary — but, in furnishing our imagination, it is legitimate to focus on episodes that have resonance for our memory because of O'Connell's extraordinary commitment to these exceptional and important values. From the many creative "signposts" in his career, where O'Connell manifested such commitment to liberty, two might be referred to here, for celebration and remembrance in the light of our current preoccupations. O'Connell, as Conor Cruise O'Brien has recently observed, was "both a strong Catholic and a strong liberal".[13] This unique combination for his time is demonstrated in his advocacy of complete separation of church and state and in his espousal of the cause of black slaves in America.

In 1807, O'Connell first propounded his unorthodox views on religious freedom at a meeting of Catholics in Dublin when he said that he would place Catholic claims "on the new score of justice — of that justice which would emancipate the Protestant in Spain and Portugal, the Christian in

Constantinople".[14] O'Connell supported Jewish Emancipation on these grounds, as he made clear to Isaac Lyon Goldsmid in September 1829:

> To my mind it is an eternal and universal truth that we are responsible to God alone for our religious belief and that human laws are impious when they attempt to control the exercise of those acts of individual or general devotion which such belief requires. I think not lightly of the awful responsibility of rejecting *true belief* but that responsibility is entirely between man and his creator, and any fellow who usurps dominion over belief is to my mind a blasphemer against the deity as he certainly is a tyrant over his fellow creatures. [15]

In the following year, when the French Revolution of 1830 overthrew the Catholic government of Charles X and substituted the apparently liberal and anti-clerical regime of Louis-Philippe, O'Connell hailed the complete separation of church and state. When revolution occurred in the Papal States in February 1831 and a provisional government decreed the abolition of the temporal power of the Pope, O'Connell rejoiced that "an adulterous connection" was broken.[16] In 1837, O'Connell was on the liberal side of the Spanish civil war against the "traditionalist" forces of Don Carlos and he hoped "the unholy union of Church and State" would be permanently severed there and in all countries where Catholic people were in the majority.[17]

O'Connell resolutely opposed bringing "the law to the aid of his creed". The prevailing view of the Catholic Church, in O'Connell's time, was that a Catholic government must assist and protect the Church. Where possible, agreements were made by the Catholic Church with Protestant governments for the regulation of the Church in such matters as the appointment of bishops. The Irish Catholic bishops accepted this position in 1799 but reversed their decision in 1808, in respect of a government veto on the appointment of bishops. Rome continued to support a government role in such appointments. It was only in 1965, with the *Declaration on Religious Freedom*, that the Catholic Church rested the concept of religious freedom upon the natural rights of persons and groups.

The second "epiphany" of O'Connell's committed liberalism is his stance in favour of black people's freedom from slavery. His cosmopolitan approach to liberty embraced the widely differing causes of the Tolpuddle Martyrs, Poles under Tsarist rule, independence in Latin America, Jewish Emancipation, liberalism in France, Spain and Italy, the peasants in India and, most striking because most costly to him, liberty for Negro slaves. He was uncompromising in his hostility to slavery, even at the loss of very considerable American support for the Repeal cause. He clashed with the Young Irelanders on this issue of principle, clearly revealing their reactionary strain of romantic nationalism: "I want no

American aid if it comes across the Atlantic stained in Negro blood," O'Connell declared in the Repeal Association in March 1845. O'Connell's powerful Cincinnati letter of 1843, combating the racialist ideas of the Cincinnati Repeal Association, is one of the great documents of O'Connell's life and of the Irish liberal tradition.

In these two ways, O'Connell "signposts" liberty: domestic and international liberal patterns of behaviour which we have yet, as a people, to live out fully in our political life. From the late eighteenth century there emerged, under O'Connell, a liberal and radical tradition within Irish Catholic political thought. O'Connell was *not* alone in his liberal Catholicism: Thomas Wyse, Thomas Moore and Bishop James Doyle — the famous JKL — though very different characters in the Catholic pantheon of liberty were as remarkable in their own way, as O'Connell, for their liberal commitment.

Thomas Moore celebrated the link between "liberty" and the Catholic Church memorably in his "The Irish Peasant To His Mistress": "Where shineth thy spirit, there liberty shineth too!" Moore adopted a Gallican position urging independence for the Irish Catholic Church from Rome's influence; he, like other liberal Catholics, wished to emphasise that Catholicism was consistent with the best feelings and principles of political liberty. Hence Catholics should "exchange the rescripts and bulls of Rome for the blessings of a free Constitution", as he put it in his *Letter to the Roman Catholics of Dublin*, published in 1810.

JKL's *A Vindication of the Religious and Civil Principles of the Irish Catholics*, published in 1823, had a comparable impact on the Irish Catholic movement as Thomas Paine's *Common Sense* had on the morale of the Americans in 1776.

Bishop Doyle declared his love for the British Constitution because of his European experience with oppressive regimes. In his *Vindication*, he compared the Irish Catholic experience of history with the Biblical experience of the Israelites: Irish Catholics look to the Constitution "...as the Israelites sighed for their country, when on the banks of the Euphrates they hung their harps upon the willows and sighed, and wept, as they remembered Jerusalem." Doyle challenged "the essential Protestantism of the Constitution" and argued that Catholics had accepted the revolutionary changes in the relationships between rulers and ruled which had occurred since the seventeenth century. Liberal Catholics in Ireland might be accused of adopting Enlightenment ideas because they were obviously useful in arguing for greater toleration and in promoting a *rapprochement* with liberally-minded Protestants. They were nonetheless sincere for seeking this common ground. It could be equally argued that men like Doyle desired to effect a reconciliation between contemporary thought and Catholic practice and doctrine: they read "the signs of the times" theologically as well as politically.

Lest Doyle be seen as an exceptional prelate the future archbishop, John MacHale (who was inspired by Edmund Burke), in his famous "Hierophilos" letters in the early 1820s, attacking Protestantism, maintained that Catholic doctrine was not "incompatible with true liberality". MacHale stressed that Catholic doctrines were "a moral obligation" and that "there is no question of the application of physical force or civil enactments" to support them. He argued for British liberties for Irish Catholics, defining civil liberty by quoting Blackstone: "civil liberty...is no other than natural liberty, so far restrained by human laws (and no further) as is necessary and expedient for the general advantage of the public."

These liberal Catholics and O'Connell's Catholic Association in the 1820s were at the forefront of constitutional development not only in Britain and Ireland, but also in Europe. The creative influence of Irish politicians like O'Connell on the evolution of British constitutional practice is often forgotten and it is assumed that Ireland was simply a recipient of a constitution evolved without any Irish contribution. From O'Connell's time we may date the conflict over perceptions of civil and religious liberty in modern Ireland, personalised in the clash between O'Connell and Henry Cooke. Cooke's concept of liberty was rooted in the Protestant reformers' rejection of Catholicism as inherently authoritarian. Cooke had a religiously informed view of liberty as enshrined in the Westminster Confession in contrast to O'Connell's secular and Enlightenment concept.[18]

LIBERAL CATHOLICISM: A NOVEL CREED

It requires an effort of imagination to recall how novel, recent and, indeed, disreputable were the origins of the term "liberal" in O'Connell's day. In contemporary Ireland, the term "liberal" retains its novel and cutting-edge quality because liberal values and issues are at the heart of our unresolved political dilemmas. The political term "liberal" was coined in Spain. "Liberal" was originally used to designate a faction in the Spanish *Cortes* after 1812 which sought a constitution. The term "Liberal Catholics" was first employed towards the end of the Restoration period (1818-29) by the journalists of the liberal *Le Globe* in order to describe their colleagues of the Catholic *Correspondent* who sympathised with liberal ideas. These represented those Catholics who were seeking to come to terms with new political ideas: personal freedoms instead of arbitrary force, political liberties arising not from privilege but from legal rights, the right of peoples to political self-determination, liberty of press and religion and possibly separation of church and state.[19] In England, the term was at first usually used in its French or in its Spanish form, and we hear from the 1820s scathing references to "English *libéraux*" or "English *Liberales*". It was not until the middle of the century that the term was really accepted in England as English and respectable.

From the 1860s, it took on the very specialised meaning of referring to members of Mr Gladstone's party. It is noteworthy that it was only in the 1880s that Gladstone paid his public tribute to O'Connell's formative influence on his own development and on that of liberalism in general.[20] In Europe, liberalism never had such a specialised meaning as that of the Liberal Party in Britain and it was variously employed.

The core of this new political faith called "liberalism" was a belief that progress, leading to the most perfect arrangement for society, could be achieved by means of "free institutions" which would be enjoyed by all people, of all classes, creeds and nations. Ideas about "free institutions" evolved, based on the many French constitutions of the Revolutionary period and on the unwritten British Constitution. Liberalism, in the decades after the French Revolution, therefore, was a new creed and many liberals were anxious to deny all connection with the violent excesses of the French Revolution. Few liberals would want to subject the individual to the oppression of the masses or to advocate "revolution" on the model of the French experience in the 1790s. The English liberal tradition was more rooted in political developments in the past than was the continental tradition; it posited a collection of liberties descended from Magna Carta and culminating in the Glorious Revolution and the assertion of parliamentary supremacy. In contrast, French and continental liberals drew more direct inspiration from the Enlightenment and its belief in the perfectibility of man given the right surroundings, particularly "free institutions".

These "free institutions" were a freely elected parliament to deliberate upon the laws, a government dependent upon that parliament to carry out the laws, and a judiciary entirely independent of government and parliament to deal with offenders against the laws. Liberals demanded freedom of speech, of religion, of the press, of assembly, the right to enter careers upon merit and to hold property with security. They sought freedom from arbitrary arrest and government based on the rule of law. These institutions and freedoms would enable the individual to find his fullest expression and would encourage society to evolve with harmonious relationships. The fundamental postulate of liberalism was that value inheres ultimately in the satisfactions and realisations of the human personality. Persons are ends not means. We have recently witnessed in South Africa, Eastern Europe and the Soviet Union great new liberal revolutions as people rise up to demand these very freedoms and institutions. O'Connell the Liberator has lessons indeed for Nelson Mandela.

WHAT HAPPENED TO THE O'CONNELLITE HERITAGE?

Brian Farrell has correctly observed that O'Connell "marks the true beginnings of the modern Irish political tradition".[21] Despite the might of the countervailing traditionalist forces, liberalism did not disappear but proved tenacious in Irish politics and has remained a potent force, if not always a successful one, in Irish Catholic politics.

The century broadly between 1860 and 1960 marked the apotheosis both of nationalism and of a conservative Catholicism in Ireland. In these circumstances dominant political aspirations were derived from the irrational and the emotional, from theology and from tradition, rather than from rational political ideas. When we designate aspirations as irrational we may think of them as strong impulses to conservatism or to reaction which could not be dignified as clear, thought-out political ideas: in Lionel Trilling's memorable phrase they are "irritable mental gestures which seek to resemble ideas". An example taken at random is "Up Dev!" as a slogan or similar civil-war-orientated slogans which dominated Irish politics until the 1960s. Liberalism, in a sense, was present as a vital part of the structure and culture of United Kingdom politics rather than as part of the visible edifices of Irish politics. Nationalist movements, like those of Home Rule and Sinn Féin, unconsciously adopted liberal parliamentary methods and arguments and used them to achieve nationalist aspirations. Liberal ideas were always in danger of being taken for granted by the parliamentary nationalist movement. The result was that Irish liberalism, as a separate political philosophy, became retarded in terms of its contemporary development. Yet the tradition of O'Connell's virtual shadow democratic government (as opposed to the British government of Ireland) and its non-sectarian character — a key liberal creation — in effect largely triumphed in 1923 when civil war ended in the Irish Free State.

The career of Michael Davitt, one of the finer spirits of Irish politics in our period, is instructive. Davitt was for most of his life an orthodox and practising Catholic; he was completely free from sectarian feeling. He, too, believed that the church should be separate from the state. Davitt underwent a long process of disillusionment with, and disengagement from, Fenianism culminating in his final break after the Phoenix Park atrocity in 1882. Davitt's ultimate political vision was of a regenerated Ireland based on land nationalisation from which the whole working population would benefit; it was to be achieved through democratic means. His 1882 reform programme, aside from state ownership of land, might be described as largely "O'Connellite". Davitt co-operated fully with Parnell in the "liberal alliance" and the struggle for Gladstonian Home Rule. In 1882, he entered parliament and was an MP for much of the 1890s. His humanitarian and international commitment reflects a great deal of the O'Connellite heritage. As T.W. Moody astutely observes, Davitt "was a man with an unquenchable interest in ideas".[22] In this respect he is exceptional amongst modern Irish political leaders.

From 1882 then, Davitt, like O'Connell, was a radical reformer, working for great social and political improvements in instalments and by constitutional means. Like O'Connell he loathed terrorism as he made clear in a letter of 25 March 1883:

> Principles of reform intelligently and fearlessly propagated are far more destructive to unjust and worn-out systems that dynamite bombs, which only kill individuals or knock down buildings but do no injury to oppressive institutions....The dynamite theory is the very abnegation of mind, the surrender of reason to rage, of judgement to blind, unthinking recklessness.[23]

Davitt's "Ireland", like O'Connell's, was no romantic abstraction but was flesh-and-blood people. Davitt's own summary of O'Connell's achievement is highly significant:

> Ireland has never produced a greater man than O'Connell, and Europe very few that can truly be called his equal in the work of uplifting a people from the degrading status of religious and political serfdom to conditions of national life which necessarily created changes and chances of progress that were bound to lead on to the gain of further liberty.[24]

LIBERAL THOUGHT IN TWENTIETH CENTURY IRELAND

By 1900, a conservative Catholic world view and an anti-modernist romantic nationalism were set fair to dominate Irish political ideology for much of this century; indeed, in Tom Garvin's phrase, this ideology became "institutionalised and even fossilised" in independent Ireland's political culture. This predominant ideology with its fear of the modern world brought Ireland to the state of almost total political and economic stagnation in the 1950s. The fiction of Canon Sheehan and C.J. Kickham reflects the values of conservative farm society guarded by its Catholic priesthood. Yet as Garvin astutely notes: "Fear of the external modern world was derived in part from a very realistic perception of the frailty of the public ideology which priests and patriotic publicists had constructed." Liberal democracy remained part of the substructure of politics and indeed the nationalist ideology largely expressed itself through liberal institutions.[25]

To explain the weakness and subterranean nature of liberalism in twentieth-century Ireland, one could adduce many factors such as the outcome of the land struggle (as Davitt had prophetically realised); the intellectual poverty of those dominant within Catholic culture from Cullen to Conway, due to the general weakness of higher-level education amongst Catholic *élites*; the partition of the island, which meant that majorities could abuse minorities rather than incorporate them into political institutions; emigration facilitating conservative stability. All of those factors promoted the irrational in place of the rational in political life. Another key factor was the power of the nationalist myth of Irish history which propagated the past simply as protest, and a violent rather than a constitutional interpretation of political development.

Yet, as Garvin has noted, despite an unpromising beginning in civil war, "liberal democratic politics have become deeply rooted in Ireland."[26] Liberalism was centrally incorporated into the 1922 Constitution of the Irish Free State and is an important and vital element of the 1937 Constitution. Indeed, Terence Brown has noted that behind the prevailing conservative vision of the Irish nation, the Irish Irelanders longed for independence of mind, integrity of personality, confident possession of identity, liberality of thought and artistic self-expression. These, it was thought, would result from cultural regeneration through an Irish revival. Brown perceives here a radical humanism clouded by reaction and dogmatism. Even D.P. Moran, who believed that the Irish nation was *de facto* a Catholic nation (and that the foundation element was that of the Gael which must be the element that absorbs), assures his fellow countrymen in *The Philosophy of Irish Ireland* that the nation he envisaged would stimulate "the free and full development of every individual".[27]

It is noteworthy how O'Connell emerged in the minds of the revolutionary generation when they became critical of the nationalist/ romantic project. Eoin MacNeill, for example, had an open admiration for the achievements of Daniel O'Connell and MacNeill's writings "show a constant insistence to place O'Connell in the heart of the Irish political tradition".[28]

During the 1920s, 1930s, 1940s and 1950s, it was primarily writers who mounted the most coherent criticisms of the ruling ideology. Seán Ó Faoláin played the commanding role in seeking to bring the urgent practical concerns of Irish people to the fore in place of the romantic historical abstractions of de Valera's Ireland. It is highly significant that it was through a biography of Daniel O'Connell, *King of the Beggars*, published in 1938, that Ó Faoláin offered a radically different interpretation of recent Irish history to that which was dominant by the 1930s.

Modern Ireland, in Ó Faoláin's view, was the fruit of the democratic victories won by Daniel O'Connell. Ó Faoláin presents O'Connell as a more appropriate model for twentieth-century Ireland than figures drawn from the Celtic Twilight such as Cuchulain. Ó Faoláin's powerful critique of prevailing ideology, and of the version of history that sustained it, led to an important symposium in the periodical *Studies* in 1938 in which Professor Michael Tierney stated quite prophetically:

> In many ways the future of our political, social and educational systems must depend on whether or not we agree with what he [Ó Faoláin] has said about the significance of O'Connell.[29]

It was Ó Faoláin, in his remarkable periodical *The Bell*, which he edited between 1940 and 1946, who pointed to Ireland's future as part of the modern world and criticised "the old patriarchal rural Ireland". He wrote in *The Bell* in August 1943:

> One comes thereby back again to the final conclusion that the really terrible threat to Ireland is an intellectual one. We are not really wide-awake at all, not keeping pace at all with the irresistible movement of life.

Ó Faoláin saw Ireland as a country only at the beginning of its creative history, not as the static end-product of a violent rebellion. He perceived Ireland as a synthesis, a mosaic, a hybrid society with a valid place for British culture as well as for Gaelic culture. *The Bell* laid an important liberal basis for subsequent Irish political, social and cultural thought. As Brown observes:

> Ó Faoláin and his contributors through attending in an empirical, investigative manner to Irish realities opened windows in *The Bell* to show how much Irish life was not some absolute state of national being but an expression of man's life in a particular place, bound up with European history, geography, economics and social forces of all kinds.[30]

Ó Faoláin led the vanguard of what has become the modern liberal movement in southern Irish life and which has had revolutionary effects since the 1960s in literature, in educational policy, in the mass media, in political ideas, in legal judgements, in the writing of history, in religious life and in Irish apprehensions of the external modern world.

Conservative ideology has been under sustained attack from this liberal advance and has been forced to seek refuge in denial and defensiveness. As Tom Garvin has observed, nationalist tradition, religious traditionalism and isolationism in Ireland must "continually and openly defend their positions against cosmopolitanism and liberalism".[31] Amongst the forces which lie behind this liberal revitalisation are rising levels of education, the influence of Vatican II on Catholicism, urbanisation, the media explosion, the women's movement, involvement in Europe, and increasing Catholic links with Latin America and the Third World. There exists a new sense of Irish Catholicism as a socially directed and potentially liberating and radical force in society. The Irish-Enlightenment responses are indeed now engaged more equally with the Gaelic-Romantic responses to the modern world than ever they were in the century from 1860 to 1960.

CONCLUSION: LIBERAL LEARNING

There exists a traditional lack of understanding of liberalism in Irish Catholic circles. Liberal Catholicism seems a strange, even a contradictory, conjuncture to many. Seamus Deane, for example, in a recent essay on "Edmund Burke and the Ideology of Irish Liberalism" totally ignores liberal Catholicism describing "the dominant liberal tradition in Irish political thought" as stemming from late seventeenth-century writers such as Molyneux, to Burke and the United Irishmen and then, inexplicably, jumping to James Connolly and Liam Mellows.[32]

The crucial Irish political questions in the 1990s, given the religious adherence of the majority of the people on the island, concern the future of liberal Catholicism. Seán Ó Faoláin talks, in the last chapter of *The Irish*, about the children, and even the grandchildren, of the 1916 generation setting out "to make liberty viable in terms of the modern commercial and industrial world". As he wryly observes, it is a process that has not been universally approved. Traditionalists in church and state cling devotedly to the old pieties, as Ó Faoláin says, "as lovingly as the ivy that chokes the growing tree".

I have suggested that on this quest or journey towards liberty there exists a protean Irish Catholic lineage for those who choose to be liberals in the 1990s. It takes, of course, exceptional politicians to promote an extension of liberty and to be prepared to take the risks such liberty always entails. When one has listed Seán Lemass, as Taoiseach, Garret FitzGerald throughout his career, Declan Costello in the 1960s and 1970s,

Conor Cruise O'Brien since the early 1970s, Mary Robinson and Dr Noel Browne, one has virtually exhausted the category in the Republic of those with a Catholic background.

Despite the lineage of liberty which can boast of names like O'Connell, Davitt and Ó Faoláin, one rightly speaks of the comparative failure of liberalism as a political creed in modern Ireland. There are many reasons, as I have suggested, for this relative failure. As Ó Faoláin observes, "Irish political thought is, to this day, in its infancy." It took a unique official censorship, between 1929 and 1967, to sustain for decades a bankrupt national ideology during which, in Ó Faoláin's words:

> ...our sails sagged for a generation; we lived under the hypnosis of the past, our timidities about the future, our excessive reverence for old traditions, our endemic fear of new ways, of new thinking, the opiate of that absurd historical myth, and the horror of the feeling of solitude that comes on every man who dares push out his boat from the security of his old, cosy, familiar harbour into modern seas.[33]

Within Catholicism, in respect of the Irish liberal quest, there remains a remarkable under-utilised resource: the *Declaration on Religious Freedom*, significantly entitled *Dignitatis Humanae*, of 1965. This vital product of the Second Vatican Council ushered in a new era in the relations between the People of God and the People Temporal; in effect, it endorsed the liberal Catholic position held a century-and-half earlier by O'Connell.

According to this *Declaration*, the dignity of man consists in his responsible use of freedom, so there must be no coercion: religious freedom is a human right. People must be free from interference in leading their lives according to their conscience: "religious freedom must be given such recognition in the constitutional order of society as will make it a civil right" and, in fact, it is the duty of the state to protect the rights of all believers and non-believers. *Dignitatis Humanae* points to the harmony which should exist "between the freedom of the Church and that religious freedom which must be recognised as the right of all men and all communities and must be sanctioned by constitutional law". The Kingdom of Christ is to be built by "bearing witness", using no methods contrary to the spirit of the Gospel. It could be demonstrated that the Vatican Council of 1965 implicitly recognised the inherent rightness of the church-state relationship which the American Catholic Church had long experienced.

As Rev John Courtney Murray, SJ, wrote soon after the 1965 *Declaration*:

> The Church does not deal with the secular order in terms of a double standard — freedom for the Church when Catholics are in a minority, privilege for the Church and intolerance for others when Catholics are a majority.[34]

Numbers have no relevance to rights: Irish liberals have been slow to build the positive case for liberalism based on Church teaching. Louis McRedmond has observed how strange it is that in Ireland "there has been no pastoral instruction on implementing the Declaration [on Religious Freedom], no apostolic letter setting out the norms to be observed."[35] The starting point for a debate on the relevance of the *Declaration on Religious Freedom* in the Irish context might be the *Submission to the New Ireland Forum from the Irish Episcopal Conference, January 1984* (Veritas, 1984), the *Report of Proceedings*, 9 February 1984 when the Irish Episcopal Conference met the New Ireland Forum, and Desmond M. Clarke's impressive critique, *Church and State: Essays in Political Philosophy* (Cork University Press, 1984).

The Vatican Council's voice ought to be a powerful buttress for Irish liberal Catholicism. Elsewhere it has proved to be the opening chapter in a great liberating movement in theology. We still have to frame the appropriate theological questions in Ireland in terms of liberty. The advocacy of liberalism in recent decades in Ireland has been shallow and anaemic, leaving it open to traditional opponents to characterise liberals as self-indulgent or indifferent, even as mere hedonists. Too readily have we accepted the idea of the terminal decay of liberalism which has so long been touted by Western intellectuals who themselves enjoy their liberal freedoms. In fact, where they have been established, liberal values and institutions have never been less under threat and where they do not exist they have never before been desired so widely throughout the world. Liberal principles are the main resource in the clash with fundamentalism of all sorts throughout the world. If positive political development is to become the norm for all religious groups who share this island, there must be consensus based upon shared definitions of liberty. For many this will mean forfeiting traditional emotional and romantic concepts but there can be "no cheap reconciliation" to use Alan D. Falconer's phrase.[36]

It is not only in Ireland, however, that the battle for liberal values within Catholicism is joined. A leading Catholic politician in the United States, Governor Marion M. Cuomo, has explored the relationship between his Catholicism and his politics as a

> ...Catholic who holds political office in a pluralistic democracy — who is elected to serve Jews and Muslims, atheists and Protestants, as well as Catholics...[who] undertakes to help create conditions under which *all* can live with a maximum of dignity and with a reasonable degree of freedom; where everyone who chooses may hold beliefs different from specifically Catholic ones — sometimes contradictory to them, where the laws protect a people's right to divorce, to use birth control and even to choose abortion.

Cuomo points out that to ensure Catholics their freedom "we must allow others the same freedom, even if occasionally it produces conduct by them which we would hold to be sinful". All religiously based values do not have "an *a priori* place in our public morality". Catholics are called to live their faith in daily life according to Church teaching, not to vote *en masse* specific and controversial Church teaching into the civil law; they are free to build a consensus in society for values they cherish. Echoes from Ireland of John MacHale's "moral obligation" but no "civil enactment" would be welcome as well as strategically important for a Catholic politician who has the calibre to be a future President of the United States. The Christian faith is not lived out as part of a constitutional *status quo*; it should be kept independent of political institutions in order to retain for each church its prophetic independence to proclaim the Gospel freely. Christian values should not and do not require a statute to uphold them. Cuomo concludes:

> We can be fully Catholic; proudly, totally at ease with ourselves, a people in the world, transforming it, a light to this nation. Appealing to the best in our people not the worst. Persuading not coercing. Leading people to truth by love. And still, all the while, respecting and enjoying our unique pluralistic democracy. And we can do it even as politicians.[37]

Contemporary realities force political parties, and even churches, to learn from history or take the consequences. In the New Ireland Forum *Report* of 1984 it was admitted, in a key and remarkable statement, that a new constitution, which would recognise the composition of the peoples on this island "would contain clauses which would guarantee civil and religious liberties to all citizens of the state on a basis that would entail no alteration nor diminution of the provisions in respect of civil and religious liberties which apply at present to the citizens of Northern Ireland". During the 1980s, however, in two referenda those who wished "to bring the law in aid of their creed" prevailed over liberal forces in the Republic. 1990 was the twenty-fifth anniversary of the *Declaration on Religious Freedom* and perhaps it is due time it was taken seriously as indicating how the Gospel should be proclaimed and lived out in a free society.

Because our history has been largely conceived as an ever-recurring cyclical pattern, it is true that few countries have understood or interrogated its past as poorly as Ireland or have paid such an enormous price for an impoverished concept of history. Pointing this out in his major work, *Ireland 1912-1985*, Joseph Lee condemns the historians who might have helped policy makers learn from the past: "It is curious," says Lee, "how little investigation historians have conducted on the theme of learning from history."[38]

It will require both imagination and generosity to evolve "free institutions" on this island which will command the respect and allegiance of all traditions. We need re-vision of our past if we are to overcome division. In furnishing our imaginations and values, an appreciation of the neglected Irish liberal Catholic tradition seems to be vital. History provides a resource for present and future attitudes which can either be liberating or oppressive depending on which elements of our past we choose to cherish. We *can* choose to cherish the memory of those who sought to extend political, religious and social freedom to all.

5

THE IMAGE IN ENGLAND:
THE CARTOONS OF HB

James N. McCord

We have become accustomed to the idea that a politician's public image — the concept or impression created in the minds of the public about a particular person — can directly affect that individual's position, power and effectiveness. Before the widespread use of photography or even engraved illustrated journals, singly-issued caricatures could play an important role in creating, delineating, or, more commonly, projecting an unfavourable impression of public figures.[1] For the decade and a half in which Daniel O'Connell sat in the imperial parliament, the most important political caricaturist was John Doyle — known to his contemporaries only as HB — a monogram created by a junction of two "IDs" one above the other, "I" being a conventional initial for John. Consequently O'Connell's image in England, specially among English politicians of the 1830s and 1840s, owed much to the work of HB.

John Doyle (1797-1868) was trained as an artist in Dublin and came to London in the early 1820s. There he painted horses and portraits but soon established his reputation through likenesses of public men published as lithographs.[2] Because of Doyle's desire to remain anonymous and to retain his political independence, his prints were popularly referred to as the sketches of HB. The secrecy also stimulated interest in them.

Doyle's politely phrased, but razor-sharp commentaries were expressed with a finesse in draftsmanship that exploited the freedom and subtlety of line made possible by the relatively new process of lithography. Most of his prints were numbered in the series entitled *Political Sketches*, published by Thomas MacLean (1788-1875) of the Haymarket, the leading print-seller in the early Victorian years. These caricatures eventually ran to some 900 prints between 1829 and 1851, appearing initially in batches of four or five, selling for two shillings each. Later they were bound in volumes of fifty or a hundred with a "key" listing the main characters in each print. A more detailed *Illustrative Key* appeared in 1841 and another in 1844, together covering numbers 1 to 801.[3] These "keys" are the primary sources of interpretive studies of Doyle's caricatures.[4] Although Doyle would have preferred to have made a living as a portrait painter, the success of his caricatures, begun at first in sport, allowed him to live respectably (just off Hyde Park) and to raise a large family. In turn, several of his children became well known for their own association with the arts: Richard Doyle (1824-83) was best know for his work in *Punch*; Henry Doyle (1827-97) became Director of the Irish National Gallery; and HB's grandson was Sir Arthur Conan Doyle (1859-1930).

Doyle is an important resource for the physical appearance of many politicians in the early Victorian era. As Norman Gash has observed in the case of Sir Robert Peel: "For the actual appearance of Peel in the eighteen forties...the most faithful impression was recorded not in any painting but in the innumerable sketches of the cartoonist H.B.".[5] Doyle's contemporaries also recognised his talent for accuracy. Thomas Babington Macauley spoke of "that remarkably able artist who calls himself HB", and *The Times* ranked him with the best of Gillray: "The excellence of these sketches is that without extravagance they give a striking and fanciful portrait of every available circumstance in political life."[6] They provide, as *The Times* also noted, "a kind of running commentary on the political events of this country".[7] They were widely distributed, but particularly valued by those most knowledgeable about politics. In the 1830s, they became, as the *Morning Post* observed, no longer a luxury but "almost a necessary of life to political people".[8] For English graphic representation of events in political history between 1829 and the late 1840s, or roughly between Catholic Emancipation and repeal of the corn laws, the drawings of HB are essential viewing.

Doyle is also a pivotal figure in the evolution of English caricature, from the biting, often grotesque figures of the eighteenth century to the more restrained, even polite caricatures or cartoons of the Victorian era. To illustrate the difference between Doyle and his predecessors, one can compare treatments of O'Connell. Few works in the tradition of Gillray,

Rowlandson and Cruikshank appeared between the death of Gillray in 1815 and the beginning of HB's *Political Sketches* in 1829. One of the last flare-ups of the popular, coloured caricature in Gillray's manner is seen in the prints of 1828-29 by William Heath (1759?-1840), who published under the pseudonym "Paul Pry". In a Heath print of 1829, O'Connell appears as a large potato supported on the ground by "roots of evil" — labelled "Popery", "Intolerance", and "Bigotry". Gas from the potato's base escapes through the "Pope's Eye", downwards to the earth — labelled "Protestant Ground" and "Church of England Lands". The print is entitled: "A Sketch of the Great Agi. Tater". The crudeness and the anti-Catholic message are self-evident.

Leaving the vulgarity and violence of the Gillray and Heath tradition behind, HB's prints seem to suggest that politics are not a matter of life and death. He often represents a political scene descriptively with only a slight embellishment. His chosen medium, lithography, or drawing on stone, also sets his work apart from that of his predecessors; freed from having to give his drawing to an engraver, not only could he respond more quickly to political events but the soft pencilled effects of the process contrasted greatly with the sharp, often spiteful lines that could be achieved by copper-plate. Doyle himself went so far as to repudiate the term caricature for his prints, giving them no other title than that of *Political Sketches*.[9] Similarly, *The Times*, in reviewing the sketches, referred to HB as "this distinguished artist, for it would be unfair to call him a caricaturist...".[10] As noted by the *Dictionary of Irish Artists* in 1913, "the likenesses were faithfully preserved — they were hardly caricatures at all."

Reflecting on the change in caricatures between the early decades of the nineteenth century and Doyle's era, Thackeray was struck by the contrast: "How savage the satire was — how fierce the assault — what garbage hurled at opponents — what foul blows were hit — what language of Billingsgate flung!... But we have washed, combed, clothed, and taught the rogue [the cartoonists] good manners."[11] HB's prints lacked the spirit, action, and vitality of the earlier caricaturists, in the view of more than one Victorian critic. "You never hear any laughing at HB," Thackeray also observed, "his pictures are a great deal too genteel for that — polite points of wit, which strike one as exceedingly clever and pretty, and cause one to smile in a quiet gentlemanlike kind of way."[12]

Perhaps because of his own Irish Catholic background, Doyle gave particular attention to Daniel O'Connell. Doyle made him the subject of approximately one fourth of HB's *Political Sketches*. Doyle's portrayal of O'Connell contributed significantly to O'Connell's public image. Although *The Times* and others might assert that HB's sketches were "perfect and impartial", Doyle had helped, by the mid-1830s, to create a stereotype of O'Connell. Through the clever and imaginative use of symbols, metaphors, and personifications, HB turned the Irish hero into a powerful, but cunning and deceptive creature whose methods gave him the upper hand over the English politicians, especially the Whigs.

HB's first portrayal of O'Connell is a realistic likeness. He appears in 1829 in a full-length drawing, "The Three and the Deuse" (Fig. 1, No. 8), a print that refers to a short play in which the parts of three characters were all played by a single actor, Robert William Elliston (1774-1831) who also happened to manage the Drury Lane Theatre.[13] In the print, O'Connell, labelled "the Great Agitator", is accompanied by John "Honest Jack" Lawless (1773-1837), an Irish journalist, and Richard Lalor Sheil (1791-1851), dramatist and politician. The facial expression, stance, posture and dress portray O'Connell as very much the gentleman — erect carriage, out-turned feet, and hand gracefully tucked into his coat. The only exception perhaps is the umbrella over his shoulder — an item which in later prints becomes a shillelagh. HB's accuracy in conveying O'Connell's likeness can be seen by comparing it with oil portraits done about the same time.

Without the title, this print has little visual punch to it. Except for providing a good likeness of O'Connell, we gain little about O'Connell that we could not obtain from reading *The Times* or the parliamentary debates. But visual evidence has the ability to offer us insights that may not be obtainable elsewhere.

When he was still depicting O'Connell in a favourable light HB drew a cartoon on the subject of Jewish Emancipation in 1830. Entitled "Repulsed but not Discouraged" (Fig. 2, No. 63) it portrays a Jew in habitual guise attempting to push open the door into parliament while Wellington and Peel are trying to close the door against him. O'Connell gives the advice, "Agitate, friend Moses, agitate! That's the way I got in." Throughout the 1830s O'Connell was an energetic supporter of the right of Jews to sit in parliament.

Doyle's portrayal of O'Connell becomes more directed and focused by means of literary metaphors and personifications. O'Connell appears as a force created by the politicians and one that is potentially uncontrollable. In "Political Frankensteins" (Fig. 3, No. 105), which appeared in January 1831, O'Connell is the giant confronted by helpless English politicians. Attempting to arrest O'Connell's forward motion with a paper labelled "Proclamation" is the Lord Lieutenant of Ireland, the Marquess of Anglesey (Henry William Page, 1768-1854), joined by the Chief Secretary for Ireland, Edward Stanley (1775-1851; later Lord Stanley and then the Earl of Derby who served as Tory prime minister). Anglesey notes that "He walks thro' it with the greatest ease." Lord Plunket (1765-1854), an Irishman and the Lord Chancellor for Ireland, stands by with another proclamation ready in his pocket. Further removed is the Whig prime minister, Earl Grey, shouting: "He must be stopped at all hazard." Sir Robert Peel, the former Home Secretary and leader of the Tory opposition, is encouraging Grey's effort to check O'Connell. Behind Peel are Lord Brougham, the Whig Lord Chancellor and Wellington, the former prime minister. If the image of O'Connell as larger than life were not clear enough, the subtitle describes the politicians as "Alarmed at the progress of a Giant of their own Creation". O'Connell becomes a Gulliver who is barely restrained by the Lilliputians of Grey's Cabinet in Fig. 4, No. 247.

When the Whigs came into office in 1830, they made a quiet attempt to conciliate O'Connell with an offer of a high judgeship, but O'Connell kept up the agitation for Repeal of the Union. In a letter to Lord Melbourne, the Whig Home Secretary, Anglesey concluded that O'Connell was "not to be had", reflecting ruefully that in the days following Emancipation in 1829 "a few yards of title for O'Connell would have secured repose".[14] Anglesey then issued proclamations to prevent the allegedly illegal meetings sponsored by O'Connell and his supporters. But O'Connell succeeded in outwitting the authorities.[15] In "Political Frankensteins" (above, Fig. 3) a person at the crowd reminds Peel that "you may cheer people on, Mr. P---, to combat this monstrous antagonist which you yourself have been mainly instrumental in rearing to his present huge proportions when you might have stopped his growth with a few yards of silk." The point being made is that Peel, as Home Secretary on the passing of the Catholic Emancipation Act, might have allowed O'Connell to be made a K.C., an honour deliberately withheld from him despite his great reputation at the Bar.

References to O'Connell's tail are another recurrent theme in HB and refer to the some thirty MPs who were supposedly attached to O'Connell.[16] The tail was a new phenomenon at Westminster and was frequently the subject of condemnation by contemporaries and by later historians. Elie Halevy, the French historian, described it thus:

> He [O'Connell] was in reality the national hero of a foreign people. His relatives — four O'Connells were returned in December 1832 — and his followers drawn indifferently from every rank of society, and having no other programme than obedience to the orders of the great demagogue made up a group — the "O'Connell's tail" — who were a clan rather than a political party and constituted a species of foreign body lodged in the entrails of the British parliament.[17]

In later prints, such as "An Extraordinary Animal" (Fig. 5, No. 383), the tail is firmly attached, implying that members of the Repeal party lacked wills of their own and were subservient to O'Connell's commands.

There was a social prejudice in England against O'Connell's "tail" which Professor MacDonagh sees as reaching absurd heights. As an instance of this he quotes from the diary of Denis Le Marchant, no Tory but an advanced Liberal and well-informed political observer:

> Daunt and O'Dwyer have more of the ruffian about them. Lalor shows that he has never been in gentlemen's society before....Some of the others are not a whit better. They are understood to subsist on O'Connell. His large house in Albemarle Street is their hotel. They live there free of expense, much, as I hear, in the savage style of their own country.[18]

A major defeat for O'Connell occurred in 1834 on his motion to repeal the Act of Union between Ireland and Great Britain. In this he acted against his better judgement but at the behest of Irish public opinion. The motion failed by a vote of 523 to 38. The fact that the Secretary to the Treasury, (the Irish) Thomas Spring Rice, who answered O'Connell's motion, was short in stature suggested the Biblical metaphor of David and Goliath (Fig. 6, No. 316). In this confrontation even O'Connell's shillelagh was no help.

The mid-1830s witnessed dramatic political changes — events that provided HB with abundant subject matter. These began in May 1834, with the resignation of four major figures in the Grey ministry — the Duke of Richmond, Lord Ripon, Sir James Graham, and Edward Stanley — over the issue of appropriating surplus revenues from the (Protestant) Church of Ireland. This was followed in July by the resignation of Grey as prime minister, and the creation of the first Melbourne ministry which William IV dismissed in November 1834. Then came Sir Robert Peel's short-lived ministry which lasted until April 1835. This period also included a general election in December 1834 in which Tories and Radicals gained while the Whigs decreased in strength, profoundly changing the political balance in the House of Commons and giving the O'Connellites added leverage. Between February and April 1835, the Radicals and Irish Repealers collaborated with the Whigs to bring down Peel's Government and bring in the second Melbourne ministry.

O'Connell's role in all of these events has been the subject of a good deal of debate among historians, but HB left his audience with no doubt. O'Connell's strength or his power, especially over the Whigs, is the major theme for a series of prints published in 1834 and 1835. From being seen as difficult to manage or as a wounded giant, O'Connell becomes the initiator of events and policies — the power behind the Whig ministry and the Whig politicians. The stereotype becomes the normal way of portraying O'Connell. Animal symbolism provides much of the method.

In early 1833 the Whig Government presented to the House of Lords the Irish Coercion Bill which, according to Dr Angus Macintyre, was "perhaps the most repressive Irish measure ever proposed by an English Government".[19] It was devised to deal with major agrarian disorder which the government blamed to a large extent on O'Connell's political agitation. It was passed by the Lords but ran into trouble in the Commons where O'Connell, aided by the British Radicals, mounted a campaign successful enough to have the bill shorn of what he considered its most objectionable features. Two of HB's cartoons on the subject are published: "Administering a Bitter Dose to a Fractious Patient" (Fig. 7, No. 244) and "Changed at Nurse" (Fig. 8, No. 253). The first shows the prime minister, Lord Grey, administering the Coercion Bill as a dose to O'Connell. The second depicts the three framers of the bill — Grey, Lord Chancellor Brougham and Lord Plunket, Lord Chancellor of Ireland — as unable to recognise the bill because of the amendments passed in the Commons. Nevertheless Plunket urges the other two to accept the amended bill. O'Connell looks on with mischievous satisfaction.

HB portrayed the Whigs as dupes or victims of a manipulative O'Connell and even more pointedly as O'Connell's captives. The Lichfield House Compact of Whigs, O'Connellites, and Radicals — or the Whig alliance as it was grandiosely known in Ireland — provides the occasion for several sketches. In a print published in January 1835, entitled "Coalition" (Fig. 9, No. 367), O'Connell is portrayed as a wolf in sheep's clothing. He is approaching members of the first Melbourne Government — Lord John Russell, Lord Spencer (previously Lord Althorp), Melbourne, and Durham — saying "Let us merge all our trifling differences and make common war on these tyrannical watchdogs!" In the background is William IV as the shepherd with Wellington and Peel as the watchdogs. The fable implies that once the dogs have been subdued, the destruction of the sheep would follow. O'Connell is shown with the mark of a skull and cross-bones, a reference to a report, at least partly true, that O'Connell had said that every man who failed to vote for the Repeal candidates in the general election should have death's head and cross-bones marked upon his door, pointing him out to his countrymen.[20] Thereafter HB often portrayed O'Connell with this mark.

The Times (27 January 1835), whose views on O'Connell closely paralleled those of HB, greeted "Coalition" with warm praise, saying that O'Connell was "in the appropriate character of a wolf (a cowardly, savage, and cunning beast of prey)". In "An Extraordinary Animal" (Fig. 5, No. 383), published in late March 1835, O'Connell appears as a cross between a kangaroo and an opossum with an enormous tail on which are listed the names of the O'Connellites. For example, J.H. Talbot, Repeal MP for New Ross, is listed as O'Talbot. This powerful tail supposedly supports the animal which in turn keeps in its pound three Whig politicians.[21] *The Times* of 28 March 1835 described "An Extraordinary Animal" as among HB's "most ingenious productions". "The exultation of the Great Kangaroo at having bagged the small triumvirate is expressed with all the energetic glee of a poacher. The poor devils who are embagged evince a sort of embicile [sic] satisfaction, verifying the satiric poet's [Samuel Butler's] dictum.

> Doubtless the pleasure is as great
> Of being cheated as to cheat."

The skull and cross-bones frequently appeared in conjunction with another symbol associated with O'Connell, the "tribute" or "rent". When O'Connell left Dublin for London, for all practical purposes he left behind the large professional income from the Irish bar. His friends organised an annual collection for his English and Irish expenses. He had no compunction in becoming a national pensioner: "I am the hired servant of Ireland," he boasted, "and I glory in my servitude."[22] HB joined in the criticism beginning with "Voluntary Tribute" (Fig. 10, No. 418). Taken from the popular story of Gil Blas, O'Connell is shown forcefully soliciting tribute from poor Pat. Instead of a carbine as in the novel, O'Connell levels the pastoral crook of the Pope — an allusion to the use made of the priesthood for the purpose of aiding in collecting the O'Connell rent.[23]

In the early part of April 1835, both before and after Peel's resignation, HB featured O'Connell in a series of prints that warned of his vaguely disguised intentions and criticised his power over the Whigs. Moving to children's literature, HB created "Little Red Riding-Hood's Meeting with the Wolf" (Fig. 11, No. 385). Lord John Russell is Little Red Riding-Hood, standing next to a very tall wolf in a cloak who is chucking her under the chin. "It is clear that the price of the Lichfield Kennell [Russell] will hardly make a mouthful for the wolf," commented *The Times*, "whose long tail seems already prepared to trip up the smaller animal with a simple whisk..."[24] In the background is a church against which Russell has turned his back, again in the words of *The Times*, "to gaze upon Dan and listen to his destructive blarney". *The Times* concludes with a general admonition to Lord John and those who would be so adventurous: "none are so wise in their own conceit, or so unconscious of their own weakness, as forward children, whether of larger or smaller growth, and upon such provender it is that beasts of prey, biped and quadruped, principally feed and fatten." The image is explicit in Fig. 12, No. 386, which shows O'Connell as Robin Hood and Russell as Little John, fleecing the (Protestant established) Church of Ireland represented by the Archbishop of Armagh. In both "Little Red Riding-Hood" and "Robin Hood", Doyle has explicitly criticised Russell and O'Connell while simultaneously defending the Irish Church.

With Melbourne's return to office in April 1835, HB repeatedly shows

THE THREE AND THE DEUSE
(circa 1829)

"Honest Jack", The Hero of
Ballibay (John Lawless).
"The Great Agitator" (Daniel
O'Connell).
"The Little Agitator", The Hero of
Penenden (Richard Lalor Sheil).

Figure 1

REPULSED BUT NOT
DISCOURAGED
(May 24, 1830)

1. The Reverend Edward Irving, extremist Presbyterian preacher.
2. O'Connell — "Agitate friend Moses, Agitate! That's the way I got in!"
3. Brougham — "You exclude the Jew and Quaker, while the Atheist, who laughs at your oaths, obtains admission."
4. Wellington — "He must not be let in yet Peel, but if we don't take care the fellow will slip in, in spite of us."
5. The Jew — "Pray let me in! I am sure I shall behave myself as well as some whom you have admitted."
6. Peel — "I cannot let you pass, if I admit you the respectable gentleman in the broad brim and all the rest, will expect to get in."

Figure 2

POLITICAL FRANKENSTEINS
Alarmed at the progress of a Giant of their own creation.
(January 18, 1831)

Offstage: "It must be admitted that we have got business enough in hand."
Offstage: "You may cheer people on, Mr. Peel, to combat this monstrous antagonist which you yourself have been mainly instrumental in rearing to his present huge proportions when you might have stopped his growth with a few yards of silk!"
The Battle between the <u>Pealers</u> and Repealers is only just beginning.

1. Brougham — "At all hazards! I don't like the phrase, it implies danger!!"
2. Wellington — "Good Generalship may be shewn in a well timed retreat."
3. Peel — "That is right."
4. Grey — "He must be stopped at all hazards."
5. Althorp (dropping "A Bill to prohibit the growth of tobacco in Ireland").
6. Plunket — "Never mind. I have got another ready made in my <u>pocket</u>."
7. Anglesey — "He walks thro' it with the greatest ease."
8. O'Connell (holding in his right hand "Repeal of the Union" and in his left hand "Agitation within the letter of the Law").
9. Edward Stanley — "This is even worse than being <u>Hunted out of</u> Preston."

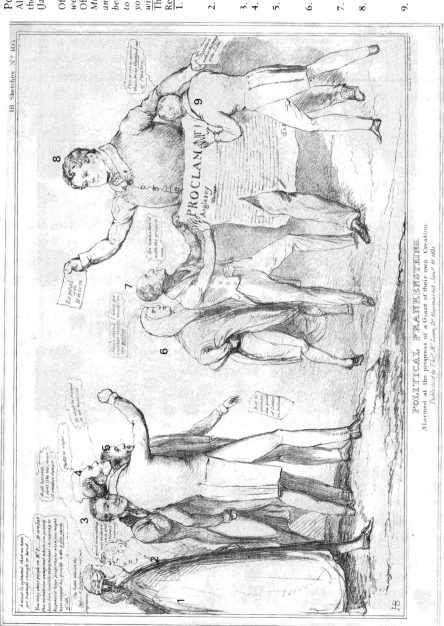

POLITICAL FRANKENSTEINS;
Alarmed at the progress of a Giant of their own Creation.
Published by Thos. McLean, 26 Haymarket, Jany. 18. 1831.

HB Sketches No. 105

Figure 3

Gulliver In The Toils Of The Lilliputians

"I was in the utmost astonishment and roared so loud that they all ran back in a fright, and some of them, as I was afterwards told, were hurt with the falls which they got by leaping from my sides. However they soon returned....."
(March 11, 1833)

1. Gulliver (O'Connell) holding Repeal document.
2. Edward Stanley.
3. Grey — *"Tolgo phonac"* (a phrase of command to fire arrows).
4. Anglesey.
5. Brougham.

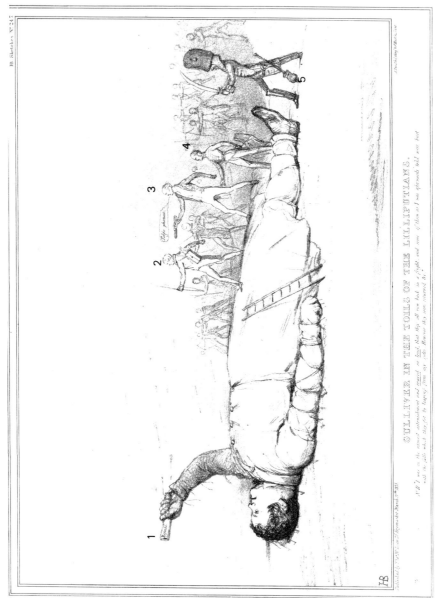

Figure 4

AN EXTRAORDINARY
ANIMAL
Neither an Opossum nor a
Kangaroo but having something of
both.
(March 26, 1835)

Daniel O'Connell as the animal;
Lord Glenelg, Thomas Spring Rice
and Lord John Russell in the
animal's pouch.

Figure 5

DAVID AND GOLIATH
(April 30, 1834)

Thomas Spring Rice "slays" O'Connell.

DAVID & GOLIAH.

Figure 6

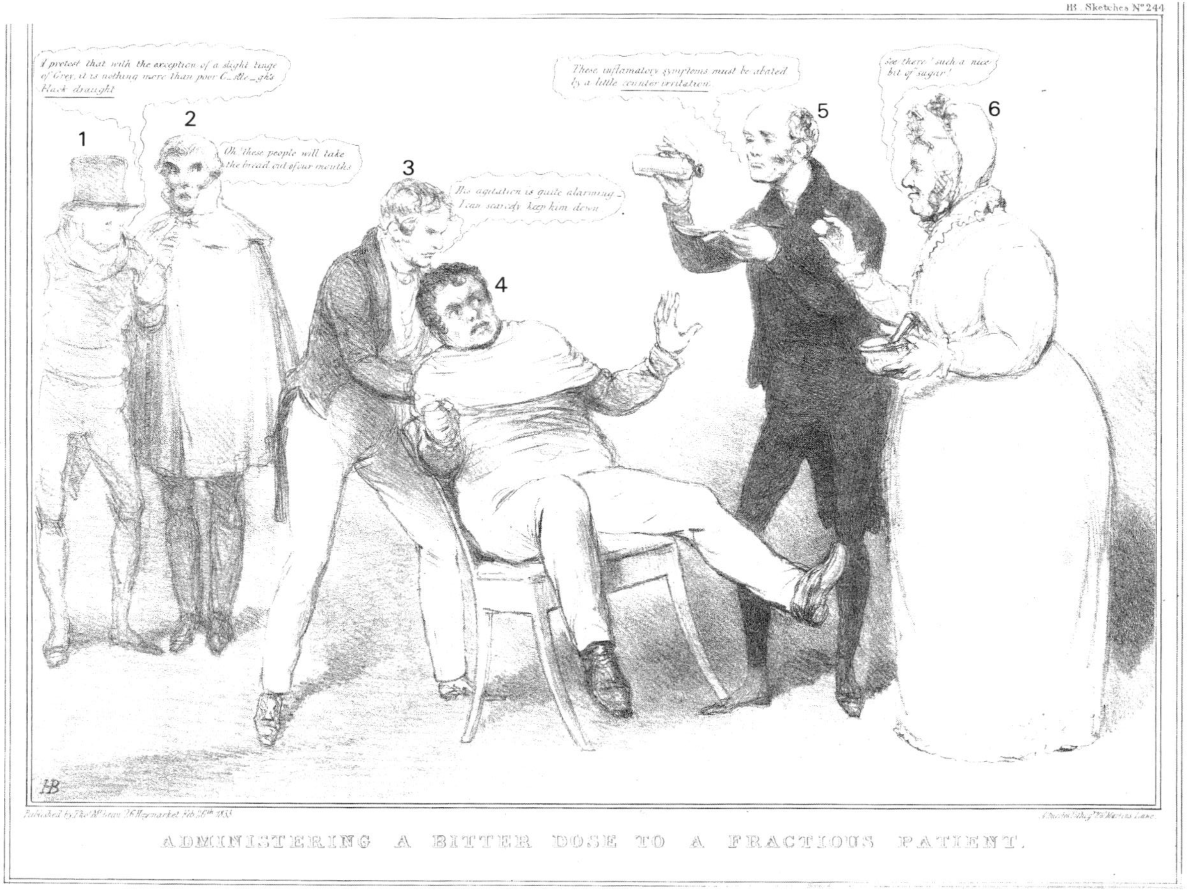

ADMINISTERING A BITTER DOSE TO A FRACTIOUS PATIENT
(February 26, 1833)

1. Eldon — "I protest that with the exception of a slight tinge of Grey, it is nothing more than poor Castlereagh's black <u>draught</u>."
2. Wellington — "Oh! These people will take the bread out of our mouths."
3. Edward Stanley — "His agitation is quite alarming – I can scarcely keep him down."
4. O'Connell.
5. Grey — "These inflammatory symptoms must be abated by a little <u>counter irritation</u>."
6. Althorp — "See there! Such a nice bit of sugar!"

Figure 7

CHANGED AT NURSE

or

"This is none of my child."

(April 4, 1833)

1. Plunket — *"Never mind, adopt it, adopt it."*

2. Grey — *"Oh this is not our Bill you must have changed our bantling at Nurse."*

3. Brougham — *"Dear me, how altered! I never should have known it as our Lamb, I hope you are not making an April Fool of us."*

4. Althorp.

5. O'Connell looks on.

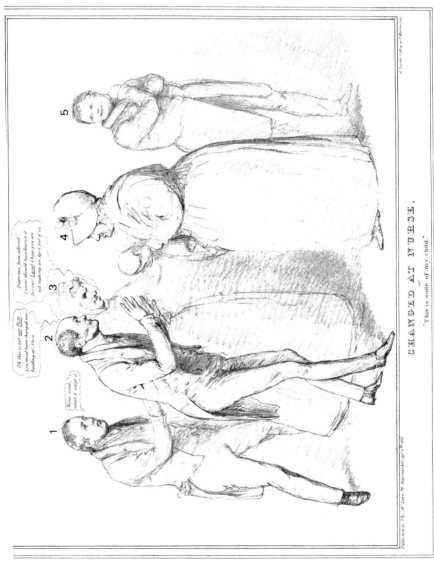

CHANGED AT NURSE,
"This is none of my child."

Figure 8

COALITION
(January 19, 1835)

1. Joseph Hume.
2. Daniel O'Connell — *"Let us merge all over trifling differences and make common war upon these tyrannical watch dogs."*
3. Russell.
4. Spencer (formerly Althorp).
5. Melbourne.
6. Durham.
7. Grey.
8. Wellington.
9. Peel.
10. William IV.

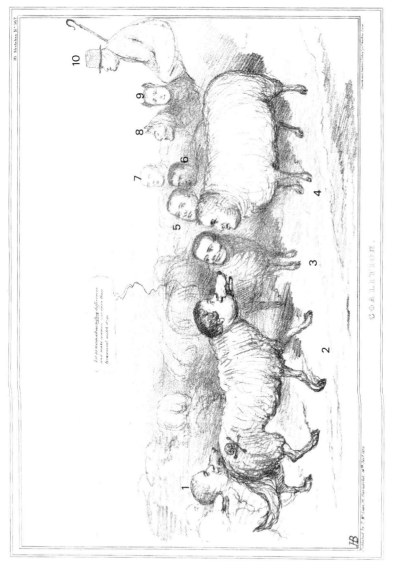

Figure 9

VOLUNTARY TRIBUTE
or
"A Passage from Gil Blas"
Translated into Irish!
(December 7, 1835)

1. O'Connell — "For the love and honour of Old Ireland, relieve the wants of a poor Patriot."

2. Poor Pat.

Figure 10

LITTLE RED RIDING HOOD'S
MEETING WITH THE WOLF
(April 3, 1835)

Lord John Russell and Daniel
O'Connell.

Figure 11

ROBIN HOOD AND LITTLE
JOHN FLEECING THE
CHURCH
(April 13, 1835)

1. Archbishop of Armagh
   [Church of Ireland] —
   *"Having been made to dance
   against my will I suppose I
   must now pay the Piper."*
2. John Russell as Little John —
   *"Lend me your purse, Master,
   and I will settle it for you."*
3. Daniel O'Connell as Robin
   Hood.

Figure 12

MERRY GO ROUND
(May 15, 1835)

1. John Russell.
2. Howick.
3. O'Connell (pushing the Merry Go Round).
4. Lansdowne — *"This is a capital hard working fellow when he takes it into his head, we are going on swimmingly."*
5. Duncannon — *"I think we ought to give him some encouragement – I say – you sir – if you go on this way, we'll...."*
6. Melbourne — *"Don't talk to him – I wonder you'd lower yourself by speaking to such an Individual."*
7. Thomas Spring Rice.

Figure 13

A Travestie
(November 13, 1835)

1. Melbourne — "All Hail, the mighty Demagogue!"
2. Mulgrave — "Health to the Prince of Gaberlunzie!"
3. Morpeth — "All Hail, King Dan!"
4. O'Connell as Macbeth.

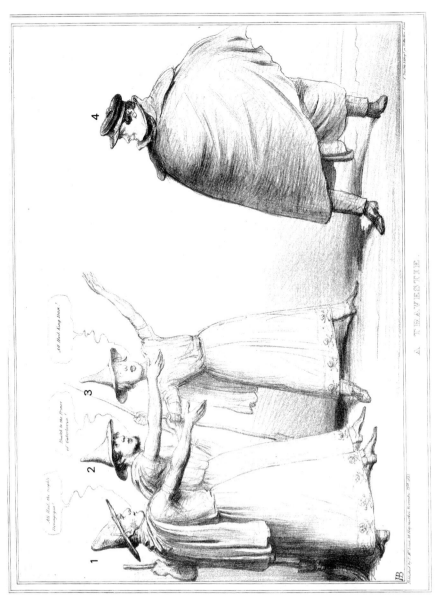

A TRAVESTIE.

Figure 14

THE REAL POTATO BLIGHT OF IRELAND.

(FROM A SKETCH TAKEN IN CONCILIATION HALL)

Figure 15

A Family Group
(Framed, glazed and ready to be
hung up at Brookes's Club)
(June 10, 1835)

Ebrington, Daniel O'Connell and
Duncannon.

Figure 16

the Whigs as dependent on O'Connell. In "Merry Go Round" (Fig. 13, No. 393), members of Melbourne's ministry are in the lucky place of riders who are indebted to O'Connell for his efforts from below. Lord Lansdowne, Lord President of the Council, praises O'Connell as "a capital hard working fellow when he takes it into his head". Lord Duncannon (1809-80; Lord Privy Seal; later 4th Earl of Bessborough), who was known to be more sympathetic to Irish questions is saying: "I think we ought to give him some encouragement" — an obvious reference to appointments or place. But Melbourne cautions them all: "Don't talk to him — I wonder you'd lower yourself, by speaking to such an Individual."[25] Melbourne had been known to speak of O'Connell as "that individual". Besides commenting on the Whig's dependence on O'Connell, the metaphor of the merry go round was that all on board were "wooden and motionless" — or so *The Times* concluded. By the later fall of 1835, O'Connell is "A Travestie" (Fig. 14, No. 416). This shows the prime minister, Melbourne, along with Lord Mulgrave, Lord Lieutenant of Ireland, and Lord Morpeth, Chief Secretary for Ireland, hailing O'Connell as Macbeth. *The Times*, referring to the three Whig ministers' deference to O'Connell as the "Weird brothers", suggested that they had lost their masculinity — "their weakness rather belongs to the gentler sex".[26]

Once we have cast a person in a particular way, as psychologists and sociologists have pointed out, we tend to keep that person in the role, whether or not that role corresponds to reality or whether or not the individual's behaviour changes over time.[27] By repeatedly portraying O'Connell as either larger than life or as the power behind the Whigs, HB reinforced the stereotype that he helped to create. By visual means, he conveyed characteristics that constituted also moral and political judgements. *The Times*, for example, thought HB had caught "The vulgar swagger and cowardly cunning" of O'Connell "with an accuracy amounting to identification".[28] In 1835, it became accepted by Whig and Tory alike, almost as an obsession, that the Whigs were dependent on O'Connell. The former prime minister, Lord Grey, in semi-retirement, protested constantly and bitterly against an alliance with "an unprincipled villain" that seemed to disgrace the fair name of Whiggism.[29] "Their [the Government's] position under the iron dominion of Mr. O'Connell is most galling to them;" reported Lord Aberdeen to Princess Lieven in the summer of 1835, "and if they have the feelings of gentlemen they must desire to escape from it."[30] It is no coincidence that in the spring of 1835 the same language was used by *The Times* in reviewing three of HB's prints that "exhibit in characters of painful truth the degraded subjection of Lord John Russell and his party to O'Connell who sometimes conquers them by 'blarney', and sometimes by intimidation."[31]

The relationship between O'Connell and the Whigs has been the subject of much historical debate and Doyle's image is very probably less than true.[32] Contrary to HB's stereotype of O'Connell's power over the Whigs, it has been argued that it was O'Connell who forfeited much of his power under the Whigs, choosing to collaborate with them and to defer to Whig leadership. The Whigs saw the collaboration as a way of returning to office but also as a way of protecting the basic institutions of the state, carrying out essential reforms, and of controlling or constraining O'Connell and middle-class radicalism.[33] They saw themselves as aristocratic leaders who could channel the popular will through a hierarchical social order and thereby bring peace to England and Ireland.[34] Wherever O'Connell's views differed from their own, the Whigs did all they could to prevent those views from influencing their governance.[35] The Whig leadership remained aloof from O'Connell, keeping social contacts to a minimum. Lady Salisbury, for example, was shocked by O'Connell's presence at the Marquess of Lansdowne's house in May 1834, "the first time I have heard of him in a gentleman's house".[36] Further, recent research has also questioned the view, widely held by HB and his contemporaries, that the appropriate clause of the Irish (Protestant) Church Bill was merely a direct response to O'Connell's wishes; it seems that the Whigs, well before 1834, were committed to reforming the Irish Church and O'Connell supported it as a means of attacking the tithes but also a way to get back into the good graces of the Whigs.[37] In their commitment to constitutionalism and reform, the Whigs and O'Connell had much in common, but contrary to the impression of contemporaries, it seems clear that O'Connell and his "tail" did not wag a Whig dog — HB's caricatures notwithstanding.

If it can be said, as Angus Macintyre has argued, that relentless criticism by *The Times* robbed O'Connell of the sympathy of informed English opinion,[38] then much the same can be said for HB. Certainly contemporaries, like Lord Lyndhurst, the former Lord Chancellor, considered cartoons as "weapons of no slight power"[39] and it was Lyndhurst who was closely associated with the *The Times'* long and intensive campaign against O'Connell.

If we accept Lyndhurst's judgement about the power of cartoons, then it can be argued that HB helped to create conditions in which the Whigs might reluctantly have to accept the appearance of being dependent on O'Connell but find it easier to make few major concessions to him — unless they were consistent with Whig policies. At the accession of the second Melbourne Government, O'Connell accepted Whig leadership, at least for the time being, suspending agitation of the Repeal question until after the Whigs fell from office in 1841. In return, O'Connell gained the appointment of a more friendly administration in Ireland, reform of the Irish corporations, removal of the tithe question, and the appointment of Catholics to a number of Irish offices — but the Whigs never supported Repeal of the Union or a number of issues favoured by O'Connell such as creating an elected House of Lords.[40]

The ways in which HB may have weakened O'Connell's influence are difficult to quantify. The constant appearance of prints during the crisis of 1834-35 kept a specific view of O'Connell before the public. *The Times*, commenting on three of the caricatures, described them as "pregnant with sound sense as well as rich humour...[they] may rouse some whom no arguments addressed to the intellects merely can touch".[41] At two shillings a print, more than three times as much as a newspaper, they appealed to a growing but still limited circle. They were produced for, and bought by, the politically articulate who could follow Doyle's commentary on topics of the moment. Between June 1834 and December 1835, MacLean published ninety-six of HB's caricatures and O'Connell figures prominently in thirty-six, well over a third of them, or on average two each month for the year and a half. Previously, in the five years between 1829 and May 1834, HB had produced a little over 300 sketches with O'Connell figuring in less than ten per cent of them. Only three other public figures received as much attention as O'Connell: the Whig leader of the House of Commons from 1834, Lord John Russell; the Irish Whig, Thomas Spring Rice (1790-1866); and Lord Morpeth (1802-64) who became Chief Secretary for Ireland in Melbourne's second ministry. "There are four persons who must live in perpetual horror of HB", observed *The Times*, "namely, O'Connell, Lord John Russell, Lord Morpeth, and Mr. Spring Rice. On these four the satirical artist has no mercy."[42]

By portraying O'Connell as larger than life and giving him an inflated importance, HB may have helped to organise public and Whig opinion more easily against O'Connell; by showing the Whigs' dependence on O'Connell, he may have helped the Whigs to be more independent. Very sensitive to the charge of being led by O'Connell, Lord John Russell certainly wanted Grey and others to know that the Whigs did not "truckle to O'Connell" as was imagined.[43] The impression of Whig dependence on O'Connell, along with the absence of any vigorous demonstration of positive support for Irish questions by the English public, may also have made it easier for the Tories in the House of Lords to be adamant in rejecting all proposals that seemed to originate with O'Connell. Evidence exists that some issues might have been settled earlier if not for the fact that they were sponsored by O'Connell.[44] For Tories, personal attacks on O'Connell became the most convenient method of discrediting the Whigs, and this became an accepted convention of political life — giving the unknown young Disraeli in 1835 valuable publicity.[45] Of course, O'Connell himself played into the hands of his opponents by his violent language, particularly against the House of Lords in his northern tour during the autumn of 1835.

In spite of HB's reputation as a "gentle" or "harmless" satirist, he contributed to a stereotype of O'Connell. As previously noted, his humorous approach was generally far removed from the vicious attacks of the Gillray or Heath tradition; or even from the views found in *Punch* (Fig. 15) of the 1840s. Nor could HB's message be compared with the anonymous letters of the young Disraeli who described O'Connell in 1836 as "a systematic liar and a beggarly cheat, a swindler and a poltroon....His public and his private life are equally profligate; he has committed every crime that does not require courage."[46] In fact, conservative magazines like *Blackwood's* complained that HB was "the tamest of the tame": "It is an evil sign to laugh at a lack of principle...to smile at errors which bring empires into peril." *Blackwood's* wanted a return to the strength of a Gillray — "he was a power to be respected and feared".[47] Even if tame, Doyle's message was clear, "The bitterest Conservative", observed the *Morning Post* in 1838, "could not make a fuller exposure of the Downing-street people and their Irish Task-master than is imagined in these sketches by HB."[48]

From a study of the caricatures one sees that Doyle was a conservative at heart. Like the *Morning Post*, Doyle's other contemporaries thought he was a Tory, well suited for the 1830s when the Whigs were in office. *The Westminster Review* asked the obvious question: "If by any accident that body of men [the Whigs] should be dismissed from their situations, and be succeeded by H.B.'s friends, the Tories — what must the poor artist do? He must pine away and die; if he be not converted, he cannot always be paying compliments..."[49] Perhaps a caricaturist by nature has to be anti-government. But judging from the caricatures Doyle seems to have become more critical of the Whigs as time passed. In fact, the early sketches of O'Connell are fairly sympathetic, revealing a kind of grudging admiration as in "The Three and the Deuse" (Fig. 1) or "Political Frankensteins" (Fig. 3), but by 1834-35, Doyle becomes much more censorious as seen in "Coalition" (Fig. 9) and "An Extraordinary Animal" (Fig. 5). Rather than being an ultra-Tory, Doyle seemed to lean towards the Stanleyite Whigs as his dedication of "The Great Boa" (No. 325) to Stanley would suggest or his sympathetic portrayal in several prints of Stanley and Sir James Graham. Like the Stanleyites who became Tories, Doyle also seemed more like a Tory, defending the (Protestant) Irish Church. The Stanleyites were unwilling to go very far in reducing the wealth of the established Church, seemingly viewing the Protestant Church as essential to protection of the monarchy and O'Connell as a threat to both. Lord Ripon, one of the Stanleyites, expected the Melbourne Whigs "to advance under the impulse of O'Connell at a rail-road Pace to a Republic".[50] Graham made the connection explicit: "Protestantism is the only weapon with which we can encounter Republicanism; we have the staff in our hand and we must lay about us, wielding the Church against O'Connell and tail."[51] As numerous prints would indicate, Doyle also seemed to fear that O'Connell's attacks on the Church would lead to the downfall of traditional institutions. After 1835, the caricatures also indicate that Doyle is a consistent admirer of the policies put forward by Sir Robert Peel.

For the Irish Catholic Doyle to take the position presented by these caricatures is puzzling, especially his criticism of O'Connell and his defence of the Protestant established Church. Little of Doyle's personal correspondence seems to have survived — he is known to have destroyed many of his original drawings for the sketches and perhaps he did the same with his correspondence. But two almost unnoticed letters to Sir Robert Peel of 1841-42 are autobiographical, almost confessional, in tone, and explain how Doyle did in fact change from Whig to Tory.[52] He was, he tells Peel, in his early political views, an "ardent supporter" of Catholic Emancipation and because the Whig party had identified with that cause, he believed they were entitled to his "respect and even gratitude". His other political views included a concern for "the undue magnitude" of the Irish Church establishment and a desire for some amelioration in the system of representation. But once the Catholic relief bill had passed, he "felt that the Catholics were bound in honour, if not in conscience, to abstain from all attacks upon the temporalities of that Establishment....I could not therefore without strong disapprobation and some shame, view the subsequent proceedings of the Catholic party, both in and out of Parliament — under the miss-guidance of Mr. O'Connell..."[53] Then when the Whigs introduced their "new and sweeping measures", he found them "imprudent and unnecessary". "From that time," he tells Peel, "my mite of influence has been opposed to popular innovation."[54]

The extensive sales of the sketches and "the importance attached to them in political circles", convinced Doyle that he possessed in his hands "an agent of some little influence". But he resolved early on to be "governed by a certain steadiness of moral and political principle" and to avoid the vulgar and crude attacks to which caricatures were so easily prone:

> This influence such as it was, I resolved should not be turned to any unworthy purpose by me, but that scrupulously avoiding all indelicacy, private scandals and party bitterness, it should — where it was not intended to amuse by some harmless jest — be directed to the furtherance of some intelligible public object, and that by such means as would by fair analogy be considered legitimate in political warfare.[55]

These letters explain aspects of Doyle's caricatures that surprised his contemporaries. *The Times* agreed with Doyle's own assessment that he differed from his predecessors in using caricatures, not as an attack on specific individuals, but as a device to convey approval or disapproval of policies and even political principles:

> As a weapon of mere personal offence, indeed, political caricature had in all ages of the world vindicated its preeminence of power; but as a political advocate — as an upholder of doctrines — as a partisan of principles — had been up to the present time almost entirely disregarded and thrown aside. Now, however, it is otherwise. Everyone who has seen the "Political Sketches" of "HB" will readily acknowledge that there is at least a possibility, through the instrumentality of the pencil, as well as through that of the pen, of carrying forward praise or blame beyond mere personalities and of making it pass on through the individual into an approbation or censure of general policy or conduct.[56]

In retrospect Doyle portrayed O'Connell in a manner that is consistent with the evolution of his political views or at least as he revealed them to Peel. He showed O'Connell primarily as a political opponent — not as some monster outside the world of English gentlemen. As *The Times* concluded about the general tendency of HB's works of art, they gave "a good-humoured turn to the dissension engendered by party feelings".[57] In fact, for the most part Doyle treated O'Connell as a gentleman — something many contemporaries were unwilling to do. A case in point was "A Family Group" (Fig. 16, No. 395) which places O'Connell in the window of the Brooks's Club with two prominent Whig politicians, Lord Ebrington (1783-1861; who later became Lord Lieutenant of Ireland) and Lord Duncannon (who served in both of Melbourne's ministries).[58] Moreover, virtually no anti-Irish racism appears in HB's caricatures — a phenomenon that reached a high point in the late Victorian era when the Irish were portrayed as ape-like creatures.[59] O'Connell is presented as a participant in the party conflict who was on the wrong side. He was shown as the Tories or Conservatives wanted to see the "Agitator" — the master or controlling genius of the Whig ministry.

Doyle's portrayal of O'Connell helped to fix and normalise a stereotype. *The Times*, the King, Earl Grey, the Stanleyites, and the Tories expected and therefore deprecated the dependence of Melbourne's administration on O'Connell. The stereotype obscured O'Connell's real contributions or achievements. Very few people recognised the calm atmosphere in Ireland in 1835-37, and even fewer gave O'Connell any credit for it. The Whigs under Melbourne, with the help of O'Connell, did much to redeem England's record in Ireland. In 1839, for example, it was possible to withdraw troops from Ireland to reinforce garrisons in disaffected areas in the north of England.[60] By creating a stereotype of O'Connell as a wolf in sheep's clothing or as a great and hungry boa with a powerful tail, HB helped to obscure the fact that O'Connell was in actuality a "domesticated animal" who worked well within the British parliamentary tradition and served as a constructive partner with the Whigs in reforming many of the basic institutions of the state. HB's use of caricatures to condemn the popular reforms of the Whigs meant that these achievements went largely unrecognised in England and were even to some extent not fully appreciated by O'Connell's contemporaries in Ireland. Depending on one's perspective, HB should be given some of the praise or blame for the failure of O'Connell to receive his just due.

6

O'CONNELL IN IRISH FOLK TRADITION*

Diarmaid Ó Muirithe

Johann Georg Köhl, a German librarian who visited Ireland a few years before O'Connell's death, considered that he had had the privilege of witnessing a rare and somewhat mysterious occurrence, the emergence of a new national folk-hero. The extraordinary thing was that the person being elevated to the status of hero was still alive, a phenomenon the German scholar tried to explain as follows:

> The Irish are a people after the old model, a people almost without a counterpart in the world. In Germany, we have everywhere become too enlightened and too self-dependent for any authority. We laugh at all who call themselves prophets; but among the Irish the old faith in saints and miracles still exists. Here alone, the mighty, the immortal and the great still find a fertile soil whence to obtain laurels and a halo. Add to this that O'Connell is an extraordinary man, a man of power, authority and wealth by means and ways hitherto unheard of in this world; and who, without employing any physical force, and without making any concessions, has, for 40 years, raised an opposition against the most powerful aristocracy in Europe, while, on his part, he has had almost nothing but a few millions of beggars as supporters.[1]

---

* Excerpts from this article were recited by the author and Dr Seán Ó Súilleabháin at the Daniel O'Connell Workshop in October 1990. This article is an amended version of the article of the same title published in Kevin B. Nowlan and Maurice R. O'Connell (eds.), *Daniel O'Connell: Portrait of a Radical* (Appletree Press, Belfast, 1984, and Fordham University Press, New York City, 1986).

O'Connell himself must have heard in his youth the various types of stories that grew around people acknowledged to be especially gifted — poets, for example — and no doubt he understood the process that made himself one of the laochra — the heroes. As one of that elite he was a product of the people's imagination, but, as has been said, imagination is not the faculty of making something out of nothing, but of using, in more or less different form, something already present in the mind. O'Connell was given the characteristics of folk-heroes of long ago; he was not deified, it is true, as Fionn was, and Cuchulainn, but some of the elements involved in the transmutation of a human into a superhuman are there nonetheless.

First of all, it was to be expected that the new hero's birth and early life should be invested with fantastical qualities. A story from Baile Mhúirne in West Cork claims that at his birth an echo was tossed back and forth between the mountains of Kerry, "so that there wasn't a man or woman who didn't know that some great thing was after happening".[2] The same story used to be told about the birth of another folk-hero, the poet Eoghan Rua Ó Súilleabháin.[3] In this instance O'Connell was made the subject of an older native tale; in other cases he became the hero of well-known international tales. He was, of course, predestined for greatness and the Almighty played His part:

> Dan's father and mother were a good few years married and no sign of a child. They were this day out for a stroll, and the rain came on them and they far from home. They took shelter in a small chapel, a miserable little hut that had a leaky roof of rushes on it. When the rain stopped they went to the parish priest to enquire why he had such a miserable mass-house. "Oh", said the priest, "the parish is too poor to provide better". "We're rich people", said old O'Connell, "and we want for nothing, and we'll give you whatever it will cost to build a new chapel". And they did. The day the first mass was said there, they were, of course, invited, and the priest asked them if there was anything troubling them or if there was anything they wanted. They said that they were childless. When the mass was being said the priest turned to the people and told them to pray now for the couple who had given them their new church, so that they'd have the child they wanted. And nine months after that Daniel O'Connell was born. And when he was born there was a cross on his back, like you'd see on an ass, and that was a sign that he'd be a famous man and that he'd emancipate the Catholics.[4]

A folk-hero should have a distinguished pedigree and according to a West Cork tradition, O'Connell was descended from Diancecht, the great physician of the Tuatha Dé Danann.[5] The first clothes the infant O'Connell wore were, so the storytellers say, passed around from house to house, as they were thought to contain great curative properties;[6] when the infant grew to manhood pieces of his cloaks were in great demand as they were thought to cure a variety of illnesses — just as did the cloaks of the kings of long ago.[7]

A folk-hero is expected to show remarkable talents in his youth, and so it is with the O'Connell of the popular imagination. A story from County Waterford says that a poor farmer once borrowed a horse from a rich neighbour and that the rich man claimed compensation when the horse was accidentally killed: the rich farmer was able to afford the services of the famous Kerry poet Eoghan Rua Ó Súilleabháin as his advocate in deciding the claim, but the poor farmer was, in the words of the story-teller, "in and out of the room and nobody could he get to help him". In desperation the poor man called a young boy who was walking to school with a bundle of books under his arm. The storyteller continues:

> He told the boy what his trouble was and the boy went into the room. Eoghan Rua said to him: "Is it you that's going to settle the price of the horse?"
> "I am," said the boy.
> "I'm in a hurry," said Eoghan Rua, "and I'll have to fix the price of the horse in three words from both sides."
> "All right," said the boy.
> "I'll have the first three words," said Eoghan Rua — "Trí fichid punt!* I've had my say. Now it's your turn."
> "Lá an Bhreithiúntais,"** said the boy, and what he meant was, that the poor man would have that much time to pay. And that boy was Daniel O'Connell. And that was how he got the better of Eoghan Rua.[8]

The important thing to remember about this story is that the child had got the better of an accepted folk-hero, a man of wit and learning and a poet of great distinction. Here, undoubtedly, was a child of promise. This victory foretold greatness as a lawyer, and as such O'Connell is imbued with another of the folk-hero's virtues, a certain malicious inventiveness in the face of overwhelming odds. O'Connell the Counsellor is a greater hero than O'Connell the Politician. Perhaps the people he led did not fully understand the complications of the political process, whereas the legal process they were all too familiar with. At any rate the stories about the great Counsellor are full of an exuberant inventiveness. One example is the story of a man who assaulted a bailiff — a hanging matter in those days. O'Connell agreed to defend him.

> "The only thing you can do," said O'Connell, "is to pretend you are dead. Here's money: go and provide yourself with a good wake." O'Connell happened to have an English visitor in his house at the time and he brought him along to the wake. They had great fun at the wake; the Englishman drank and smoked and played games and made love

---

* Three score pounds.
** The Judgement Day.

and even said a prayer for the corpse. When the case was called, O'Connell called him as a witness, and the Englishman swore that there was no use proceeding with the case: he saw the defendant dead; wasn't he himself at his wake? The case was finished there and then. A few days later didn't the bailiff meet the corpse on the road. He took such a fright that he left the country and never came back any more![9]

The story of the Doneraile Conspiracy and of O'Connell's night ride from Derrynane to Cork to defend the men involved is well known. This story has got curiously interwoven with an old Blasket story concerning the crew of a fishing boat brought from Kerry to stand trial for smuggling in Belfast, and as an example of how a folktale grows, the story is interesting:

There was a crew of a boat in Uíbh Ráthach a great many years ago and they were smuggling something in from a vessel and they were caught, of course; and they were taken to Belfast where they were to be sentenced. And it happened that some landlord came into the prison and he saw them and they complained their case to him.

"Musha, poor men," says he, "You're the pity. Is there anyone that could help you?" "There is one man," said one of them, "and if he was here, he'd speak for us."

"And where is that man?" said the landlord.

"He's in Derrynane, in Kerry, in Uíbh Ráthach," the man said, "and his name is Daniel O'Connell, and he's a counsellor and he's very good."

"Oh, God be with us," said the landlord. "He's too far away," says he, "but I promise you this much: I'll do my best for you."

He went off then, the landlord, and he didn't stop until he went to a man of his acquaintance who kept racehorses, and he had the best horse in Ireland. He offered him £100 if he'd go to Derrynane and bring Daniel O'Connell. The man took the money and he didn't draw rein until he came to Derrynane and told Daniel O'Connell the story.

"Oh, tut tut!" said Daniel when he heard the story, "I'll be too late. We haven't much time to get there." He dragged out his own horse, and off they went to Belfast. And so fast they went that when they arrived, Daniel's horse fell dead under him. Most of the case was heard by this time and things looked bad for the men from Uíbh Ráthach. But Daniel the Counsellor spoke up and he said: "I'm speaking for these men, Judge; don't give your judgement yet."

"And who are you!" said the Judge. "I can't put back the clock or reverse the law — my judgement is given", he said.

"Ambasa"[*] said Daniel O'Connell. "I'm Daniel O'Connell," he said, "and I'm a counsellor of repute, as knowledgeable as you or any judge in the place, and put your court in action again," he said, "otherwise you'll never again sit in that chair. And it isn't here the case should be heard but back in Derrynane in Uíbh Ráthach, where they

---

[*] A mild expletive.

did whatever they did."
The men were let out and taken to Derrynane, and I suppose Daniel O'Connell wasn't too hard on them. Whatever they were charged with, it wasn't very much. And I heard they were let off.[10]

As a politician and lawyer, O'Connell was, in the minds of the people, the lone Champion fighting their cause in a foreign land where his life was constantly threatened. The story of O'Connell and the Irish servant girl who warned him that a glass of wine put before him at a dinner party was poisoned, is well known; indeed a version of the conversation between them has reached the folklore of the Scottish Isles. A Munster version has it:

> A Dhónaill Uí Chonaill, a' dtuigeann tú Gaolainn?
> Tuigim, a chailín, is a mhaireann dem' ghaolta.
> Tá an iomarca salainn sa ghloinne san taobh leat,
> Mas fíor san, a chailín, is maith í do spré-se.*[11]

If one were to believe some of the stories, O'Connell had no need to fear the poisoned cup. Like another hero of old, he was invulnerable, except in the heel![12]
All great champions, of course, must prove themselves in armed combat and Dan's one and only duel wasn't enough for the storytellers. So other adversaries were invented:

> One time O'Connell had to fight a duel in London. The greatest swordsman in England was against him. He was no match for Dan. Time and time again, the Counsellor got through the Englishman's guard only to find that his sword buckled on the Englishman's chest. The Englishman was wearing a vest of armour, unknown to Dan. He'd be there yet getting nowhere only for that an Irish boy in the crowd, knowing the secret, called out to him: "A Dhónaill, conas a mharófá muc age baile!" Dan saw what was meant. He lunged at the Englishman's throat and killed him.[13]

Usually O'Connell did not have to rely on help from his friends to outwit the enemy. The phenomenal mental agility usually associated with folk-heroes took care of things. A Sligo storyteller illustrated the point in making O'Connell the hero of an international tale, *The Cat and The Candle*. To make a long story short, an Englishman bet O'Connell that his two cats would hold up two candles all during dinner. O'Connell won his bet by producing two mice from his pocket.[14]

---

*"Daniel O'Connell, do you understand Irish?"
"I do, girl, and so do all my relations."
"There's too much salt in that glass in front of you."
"If that's true, girl, you'll get a good dowry."

Many's the time, the storytellers assure us, O'Connell perplexed the Westminster Parliament with ruses and trickery. According to one storyteller he made quite an impression in his first week as Member for Clare:

> When Daniel O'Connell was going forward for election as Member of Parliament [in London], an English member said that if O'Connell sat in the House of Parliament he would shoot himself. O'Connell was elected, and the first day he sat in the House, he kept his hat firmly on his head. He was ordered to remove it, but he asked to be allowed to keep it on, as he had a bad headache. Permission was granted. Next day, he wore his hat again, as his headache hadn't improved. The third day, he wore his hat again and kept his head bent down, as he still had the headache. On the fourth day he entered the house with his head in the air, and his hat on, and everybody knew that his headache had left him. He was asked how his head was, and he said he felt fine. "Won't you remove your hat, then?" they asked him. "I won't", he replied. "Whatever passes three days in Parliament becomes law." So he kept his hat on, and did so all the time he was a member, although everybody was bareheaded. He kept looking around him, and somebody asked him, "How do you like this house?" "I like it very well", he replied, "but I'm greatly surprised that it doesn't collapse with a perjurer inside it." The man who had sworn to shoot himself heard the remark and he went out into the yard and shot himself.[15]

It is interesting that in the Rosses, County Donegal, an impoverished parish that until very recently depended on the earnings of seasonal labourers in the fields of Scotland, O'Connell the gifted public orator is best remembered. These labourers, potato-pickers and railway navvies gave O'Connell unswerving loyalty and followed him in their thousands on his triumphant tour of the Scottish cities in 1835. They became known to the native Scots as "the Dans", and to the present day, the challenge of slum children to one another in the school playgrounds in Glasgow is: "Are you a Billy or a Dan?"

These Donegal labourers in Scotland heard O'Connell speak in a hostile environment, they wondered at his courage and at his great gift of oratory, although many of them may not have understood him fully. Their children and grandchildren were told stories about the great man. A woman from Keadue in the Rosses told me, a few months before her 104th birthday, that her mother, who had heard O'Connell speak in Glasgow, insisted that "when O'Connell used to go out in his garden practising a speech, the birds used to stop their singing to listen in admiration".[16] "An fear a chuir draíocht ina luí le fuinneamh a ghlóir", was what the Waterford poet, Pádraig Ó Míleadha, called him, echoing the sentiment.*[17]

---

* The man whose strength of voice made magic.

A Kerry storyteller asserts that O'Connell's great gift of oratory came to him through his grandmother Máire Ní Dhuibh, a poet:

> The Counsellor and John Sigerson used to oppose one another in law cases and John used to say to him that it wasn't through scholarship that Dan used to best him but through poetry he got through an old hag of a grandmother he had.[18]

In many places people told stories about O'Connell's fabulous virility. Rathkeale in County Limerick stands indicted as the only town in Ireland that didn't provide a woman for his bed;[19] his mistresses were legion and they included Queen Victoria.[20] A Rathkeale man has told the present writer that he does not know whether to be proud of the town's high moral standards or ashamed of its lack of hospitality.

Even some of the stories concerning O'Connell, the great advocate, have sexual overtones. One story has it that while out on horseback near Derrynane, the Liberator overheard a dispute between some children. The dispute was resolved by a curly-haired boy who argued the case so persuasively that the Counsellor enquired of him who he was. "They say I'm a son of Daniel O'Connell", replied the boy.[21] All these stories are a product of the folk-mind. The heroes of old, on which the O'Connell of folklore is to a great degree modelled, were ever famous for their sexual energy.[22]

The storytellers did not destroy truth in their making of this new folk-hero, if they embroidered it for the sake of their art. Their stories are interesting in a hundred ways not least of which is that they are a mirror of the new democracy their subject had created almost single-handed, a democracy of hope and pride and honour. He had lifted the people from their knees and they, in return, paid him the supreme compliment of making him a hero.

Theirs, of course, was still a very vital folk-art, whereas Gaelic poetry was at the time in a state of decay. Theirs was a truly popular literature, in the best sense, whereas all the poets could do was to sing of the return of princes who had long ceased to exist, or of imminent foreign invasions, in verse that had lost its music and its magic. Reality lent nothing to Gaelic verse in O'Connell's time.

The most significant thing about the songs written about O'Connell in Irish was the attitude of the poets to the Counsellor's policy of constitutional agitation. Perhaps it was the influence of the secret agrarian societies, perhaps it was the extension of the mythology that demanded prowess in arms from a champion; in any case, the hero of Derrynane was expected to lead his people into battle. Tomás Rua Ó Súilleabháin assured his listeners that O'Connell was ready, his blood-sword in his hand:

Tá an scafaire Dónall, i bhfoirm is i gcóir
Is claíomh fola ina dhóid chun éirligh*23

Seán Ó Conaill saw his namesake with sword in hand amid the corpses of his enemies:

Ag tarraingt a chlaíomh le linn an ghábhaidh
Na conablaigh sínte do bhíd ar lár.**24

Raftery, the blind poet of the West, displayed a certain belligerence, too, in a poem called "Bua Uí Chonaill" — O'Connell's Victory:

Atá Turcaigh is Gréagaigh ag gabháil dá chéile
Agus caillfear na céadtha i bhfus agus thall;
Aimseoidh Sasanaigh agus Franncaigh a chéile
Agus lasfaidh Éire le faobhar lann;
M'impí ar Íosa, Dia hAoine a céasadh
Nár théigh mé in éag go dtige an t-am
A mbeidh gach cuid acu ag planncadh a chéile
Agus go bhfághmaoid pléisiúr ar "Orangemen".

Gunnaí is lámhach is tinte cnámha
Beidh againn amárach, agus tá sé in am,
Ó fuair Ó Conaill buaidh ar a námhaid
Aipeochaidh bláith is beidh meas ar chrainn;
I gCondae an Chláir tá uaisle is ard-fhlatha
Ag crathadh lámh is ag déanamh grinn
Acht bog faoi an gcárta go n-ólam sláinte
Na bhfear ó Árainn go hInse Chuinn.***25

* The strong man, Daniel, ready and able,
And a blood sword in his hand for slaughter.
** Drawing his sword in the fray,
Corpses strewn, vanquished.
*** The Turks and Greeks are attacking one another
And hundreds will be lost, near and far;
The English and the French will meet,
And Ireland will light with the edge of blades;
I implore Jesus who was crucified on Friday
Not to let me die until the time comes
For the lot of them to be beating one another,
And until we'll take revenge on Orangemen.

We'll have guns and shooting and bonfires tomorrow,
And it is time,
Since O'Connell gained victory over his enemies
Flowers will bloom and trees will blossom;
In County Clare the nobility
Are shaking hands and celebrating,
So send round the measure and we'll drink the health
Of the men from Aran to Inchiquin.

A song by an anonymous Munster poet describes O'Connell leading his people into battle:

> Chuala fuaim na hadhairce ar Shliabh Gaibhle le guth is greann
> Ó Conaill is a mhórshluaite go buacach ag teacht anall
> Tá bualadh ar shliabh le chéile agus lámhach ar dhá thaobh na habhann
> Is a chailín bhig na luachra, sin buaite ar chlanna Gall.*[26]

The Kerry poet, Diarmaid Ó Sé, was a realist. He saw the wretched people thronging to Kilgarvan to attend one of O'Connell's meetings and the verses he wrote on that occasion showed that he understood the magnitude of the task facing O'Connell and the helplessness of the people the great man led:

> A Rí Ghil na Rithe do chruinnigh an dream seo
> Is gur minic i dteannta iad ag taxanna a gcrá
> Is go bhféachaidh Mac Muire orthu ag titim le hamhgar,
> Is gan acu mar annlann ach brúscar na trá.**[27]

Many Gaelic songs were, as may be seen from some of the quotations above, naive and bitterly sectarian; as poetry some of them are execrable, but at least the poets sang again with gusto, in contrast to what Seamus Heaney has called "the decadent sweet art" of the poets of the eighteenth century.[28]

Many of the songs about O'Connell in English likewise contain what was thought to be dangerous, seditious material. In the spring of 1831, John Irwin, chief constable of Carrickmacross, County Monaghan, wrote to Major Darcy, the inspector general of the constabulary, reminding him of information and requesting permission to prosecute. Two of the ballads the chief constable thought treasonable were "The Repeal of the Union or The Liberation of Mr. O'Connell" and "Freedom, dear Freedom will Carry the Day". The first ballad contains the lines:

> Rejoice each patriotic brother,
> Daniel's foes have knuckled down,
> Freedom's cause will shortly smother
> Tyranny in Europe round.[29]

---

* I heard the sound of the horn of Sliabh Gaibhle,
O'Connell and his hordes coming over in victory;
The battle rages on the hill, and there's shooting on both sides of the river,
And little girl of the rushes, there's the defeat of the English.
** O King of Kings who brought those people together,
A people tormented by taxes so often,
May the Son of Mary help them as they fall from hunger,
Without food, except what the sea gives up.

The second song contained the threat:

> But think upon Belgium, sweet Poland and France,
> Where despotic knaves they soon found their graves.[30]

Perhaps what irked Mr Irwin most was a couplet that suggests that following King Dan's victory:

> Placemen and police must soon go away
> With corporate despots to go and hawk pisspots.[31]

In the same year the police at Newbridge, County Kildare, attempted to stop the public singing of a ballad that contained the vain hope that "Bony and O'Connell will set old Ireland free". This ballad was described as "a most mischievous and seditious libel" and the man who insisted that the police take action wrote that "the hawkers ought to be apprehended but it will be important not to rest there; every effort ought to be made to find out the printer, and through him the person or persons who compose and promote the circulations of such libels." The ballad singer was sent to jail. Indeed such was the hullabaloo about these ballads that the government deemed it necessary to enforce the 50th of George III, under which a strolling ballad singer might be arrested and committed to prison or the House of Correction until securities could be furnished for his or her good behaviour, or until he or she should be discharged by the magistrate. The law had little effect. The seditious ballads about O'Connell continued to be made, printed and sung. There were innocuous ballads made too, of course. "The Green Flag" is a typical example of the type composed to commemorate O'Connell's meetings. This is part of it:

> Emancipation, he has got,
> He has gained that glorious battle,
> With noble Sheil our worthy friend,
> They'll make the House to rattle,
> So Irishmen join heart and hand,
> I speak to each communion,
> And bravely join the noble Dan
> For to repeal the Union.
> Recorded then it shall be,
> And appear in future story,
> The day O'Connell he was chaired
> In triumph through Kilgory.
> Long live our good and gracious Queen
> Who granted the Reform;
> Success to Dan, that worthy man
> Who does our Isle adorn.
> Our shamrock gay on Patrick's day
> We'll wear in pomp and glory,
> And brave O'Connell wore the same
> When chairing through Kilgory.[32]

There are some amusing ballads concerning O'Connell's skills as a lawyer. The following is part of one called "O'Connell and the Irish Tinkers in London":

> When Daniel O'Connell first went to London
> He then did claim as a member for Clare
> The Cockneys all eager they crowded around him
> And the cheers of our Irishmen rended the air.
> One day through the streets as brave Dan was walking
> A party of Cockneys to view him they stood
> In order to humbug the monarch of Ireland
> One pulled out a note and said, "Sir, is that good?"
> To answer the question brave Dan was not lazy,
> The note to his fob he conveyed in a trice,
> When asked to return he says to the fellow
> "Sir, I'm a counsellor, pay for th' advice!"[33]

There is a hilarious macaronic song about a young man who claimed that creasa an tSamhraidh — the sparks of Summer — led him astray. He was apprehended by the police in Inisteogue, Co. Kilkenny, in broad daylight, pleasuring a young lady in a lane. As he departs for a long stretch at hard labour, he exults:

> But the voice of O'Connell will gain the Repeal
> Is beidh cailíní oga le fáil ag an saol.*
> With no opposition and that without fail
> Is beidh peelers gan saibhreas dá ngárlaigh.**[34]

O'Connell was satirised too, of course. His supposed fondness for the ladies is mentioned in a few songs. The conversation between the Old Woman and the Tinker seems to have been a favourite in Dublin public houses:

> On looking around me I espied a bould tinker
> Who only by chance came a strolling that way
> The weather being fine he sat down beside her
> What news honest man, this old woman did say
> Ah 'tis no news at all ma'am replied the bould tinker
> But the people will wish that he never had been
> 'Tis that damnable rogue, bould Daniel O'Connell
> He's now making children in Dublin be steam.
>
> By this pipe in me mouth then, replied the ould woman,
> And that's a great oath on me soul for to say,
> I'm only a woman but if I was near him,

---

* And everybody will be able to have young girls.
** And peelers' children shall be destitute.

I bet you my life 'tis damn little he'd say.
Sure the people of Ireland 'tis very well known,
They gave him their earnings tho' needing it bad,
And now he has well recompensioned them for it
By taking what little diversion they had.

Long life to your courage, replied the bold tinker,
And long may you live and have youth on your side,
And if all th'ould women in Ireland were like you,
O'Connell could throw his steam engine aside.
I think every girl that's in th'ould country,
Should begin making children as fast as they can,
And if ever her majesty wanted an army,
We'd be able to send her as many as Dan.[35]

O'Connell was satirised too by the Orange balladeers of the North. A ballad containing the following lines was printed by Mayne of Belfast, who displayed a singular impartiality in printing vitriolic songs for both the Catholic and Protestant factions:

By the tail on Balaam's ass it will surely come to pass,
That the rebels by the score we will put under
Then all the rebel bells from Rome to Royal Kells,
Will proudly ring out The Boyne Water.
Dan O'Connell he may boast of his great big rebel host,
He can swear they're ten million in number
But half of them you'll find, they are both lame and blind,
But we're the bould Orange heroes of Comber.[36]

Another ballad, printed by Mayne for a Catholic ballad-seller, refers to Orange rioting in the wake of an O'Connellite procession:

It is plain to the world they outstepped the law
To spill Roman blood without proper cause,
If processions should grieve them themselves should throw by
Their parading and walking on the 12th of July...

Long live our good queen I hope she'll protect
From daylight assassins her Roman subjects
And look now with justice upon our sad case
And check each disturber of the public peace...[37]

In Wexford, O'Connell took his place beside Nelson, Wellington, the Czar of Russia, the King of Poland and such traditional heroes as St George in a Forth mumming play composed in the mid-1830s. The barony of Forth is inhabited by descendants of the settlers who came with Fitzstephen in the Anglo-Norman invasion of 1169, and the people who live there retain many of their mediaeval customs and traditions. The mumming plays derived from the mediaeval morality plays, and contain a mixture of heroic declarations and dancing.

Enter Daniel O'Connell:
Here I am, the great O'Connell, from a knightly race I came,
My royal habitation lies in ancient Derrynane.
I am the man they call brave Dan, who stood your friend on all occasions
And the first MP that ever sat of the Catholic persuasion.
For my country's wrongs I deeply felt, they filled me with vexation
And our cruel foes for to oppose, I formed an Association.
'Tis certain sure, the Church most pure, should persecution bear,
But the penal yoke was lately broke, by electing me to Clare.
To parliament straight away I went, in hopes to free our nation,
Wellington and Peel, I made them yield, and grant emancipation.
The Catholic rent I underwent, to break and wreck in twain,
Those tyrant's chains, from off those plains, they bound up with disdain,
For thirty-three years, it plain appears, our rights to us denied,
They may regret they have borne away their Union as their pride.
And from that time in chains so were bound, for justice we appealed,
We swore that day that come what may to this we would not yield.
By St Patrick's sons you have laurels won, and been raised to dignity.
Our brothers' cries you did despise, and our country's misery.
So now your cause and penal laws, I'll expel by exhortation,
Those notorious tithes I'll lay aside, or in blood I'll steep the nation.
Your tyranny won't frighten me, nor your hellish emigrations.
Your infernal ends, they stood your friends, if I live I'll free the nation.[38]

When the great man died his people mourned him in hundreds of songs. It is said that over one million copies of a ballad called "Erin's King", or "Daniel is No More" were sold within a short time in Ireland and in Britain.

To Mullaghmast, likewise Tara
As a modern Moses he led us, you see,
Though we were pursued by proud and haughty
In the land of promise he left us free
A shout is gone from Dingle to Derry
Along the Boyne, the Liffey and the Nore,
And all repeat in mournful accents,
Our noble leader, brave Dan no more.[39]

But without a shadow of a doubt, the most moving tribute to the great leader was penned by a Clareman, Séamus Mac Cuirtín. It is a noble poem and it struck an apocalyptic note. It was as if death had dispersed all the old mythologies leaving a new reality in their place: the great hunger impending over a leaderless nation.

Beidh t'fheorainn áilne arís fé cháin
Ag méirligh fhallsa an imreasáin

Is sliocht na sean le fuacht is fán
'Na srutha seolta ar seachrán.*40

Gone too was the glorification of war as the Clareman reflected on O'Connell's gigantic achievement.

Ó Conaill cáidh an flaith gan bhéim
Ad startha fíor do fuair árd réim
Fíraon Fodhla bhuaigh gach clú
Gan chréacht gan chosgar, gan fuiliú.**41

What more impressive tribute could have been paid to O'Connell, the greatest of the political folk-heroes of Ireland?

---

* Your beautiful lands will again be under the yoke
  Of false, evil troublemakers,
  And the heirs of the ancient stock dispersed,
  Scattered in their thousands.
** The gentle O'Connell, the peerless leader,
  Who achieved the highest renown,
  A good man of Ireland who won every honour
  Without a wound, without destruction, without spilling blood.

7

A RESONANT TRADITION:
SOME GAELIC POETRY OF
UÍBH RÁTHACH

Paddy Bushe

In 1963 Austin Clarke published a poem, "Song of the Books", which included the following stanza:

> The Skelligs hid again their stone-steps,
> The hermit cells that had been skeps
> Of Heaven's beeswax. Thunder slept
>   In a high coombe.
> By Gallerus and Caherdaniel
> The torrents poured out. Barn, crab-tree wall
> Sheltered the house of Derrynane:
>   In lamp-lit room
> The Liberator marked a law page:
>   Outside, green gloom,
> Thick branches, glim of tideways raging
>   With heels of spume.
> A gust struck, snapping chain and rope post.
> Book-boxes of a Gaelic poet
> On board a vessel sank with side-blow.
>   A little doom.

The picture of Daniel O'Connell is attractive, the reference to the Gaelic background, with the suggestion of its demise, is evocative. But what interests me in the context of this article is that Clarke based his poem, in form exactly and in content quite closely, on a poem called "Amhrán na Leabhar" by Tomás Rua Ó Súilleabháin, a contemporary and protegé of O'Connell and to whose "little doom" I will return. It is on this aspect of the Gaelic poetry of Uíbh Ráthach I wish to concentrate, its facility for ranging back and forth in time, from mythological texts to the most contemporary of urban literature. Indeed, in Kerry parlance, it could be described as a chronological catch-and-kick type poetry in which, despite the apparent randomness of the movement, the echo always seems to land in an appropriate place.

To begin at the beginning: Robert Graves in *The White Goddess* wrote: "English poetic education should, really, begin not with *The Canterbury Tales*, not with *The Odyssey* not even with *Genesis* but with *The Song of Amergin*." This is a large claim. But let us first hear the poem he refers to: Setting his right foot on land at Inbher Scéne, Amergin made this chant:

> I am wind on sea
> I am wave in storm
> I am sea sound
> and seven-horned stag
> I am hawk on cliff
> a drop of dew in the sun
> a fair flower
> a boar for valour
> I am salmon in pool
> lake on plain
> a hill with ditches
> a word of art
> that pours out rage
> the God who fashions
> fire in the head.
> Who makes smooth the stony mountain?
> Who announces the phases of the moon?
> And who the place of the sun's descent?
> Who calls the cows from the house of Tethra?
> On whom do the cows of Tethra smile?
> Who is the force, who is the god
>   who shapes blades on a hill of sickness?
> Spear wailing,
>   wailing in the wind.

Thus Thomas Kinsella translates from the *Leabhar Gabhála* or *Book of Invasions*, a mythological history of early Ireland. The above incantation is ascribed to Amergin, one of the sons of Milesius, the first Goidelic or Gaelic invaders of Ireland, who landed near Loch Currane at Waterville or, as it was originally known, Loch Luighdech. Thus the course of Gaelic poetry may be said to have had its beginnings on the shores of Ballin-

skelligs Bay. As we have seen, Robert Graves attributes a wider importance to the poem, seeing in it what he called "the prime poetic myth". I
don't know if he was aware that his grandfather, as Bishop of Limerick,
consecrated the small church which stands within a spear's throw of
where Amergin is said to have landed.

This "mysterious runic poem of Amergin", as Benedict Kiely has called
it, has poetically nourished writers right up to our own time. Thomas
Kinsella used it as a basis for his own poem, "Finistère". This is the
concluding section:

> They fell silent. I chose the old words once more
> and stepped out. At the solid shock
> a dreamy power loosened at the base of my spine
> and uncoiled and slid up through the marrow.
> A flow of seawater over the rock fell back
> with a she-hiss, plucking at my heel.
> My tongue stumbled.
>
> Who
>   is a breath
> that makes the wind
> that makes the wave
> that makes this voice?
>
> Who
>   is the bull with seven scars
> the hawk on the cliff
> the salmon sunk in his pool
> the pool sunk in her soil
> the animal's fury
> the flower's fibre
> a teardrop in the sun?
>
> Who
>   is the word that spoken
> the spear springs
>   and pours out terror
> the spark springs
>   and burns in the brain?
>
> When men meet on the hill
> dumb as stones in the dark
>   (the craft knocked behind me)
> who is the jack of all light?
> Who goes in full into
> the moon's interesting conditions
> Who fingers the sun's sink hole?
>   (I went forward, reaching out.)

Flann O'Brien also used the poem in *At Swim-Two-Birds* but, as might be expected, in a much less serious vein:

> I am a bark for buffeting, says Finn.
> I am a hound for thorny paws.
> I am a doe for swiftness.
> I am a tree for wind-siege.
> I am a windmill.
> I am a hole in the wall.

I don't think Robert Graves would have approved.

The myth of the Milesian invaders continued in Uíbh Ráthach poetry. Daniel O'Connell's grandmother, Máire Ní Dhuibh, a famous versifier, lamented her children and nephews going abroad as "noble scions of the Soldier of Spain" according to a version in "The Last Colonel of the Irish Brigade". The soldier of Spain is of course Miles Espanus or Milesius. In a wedding poem for the Liberator's brother James, Tomás Rua Ó Súilleabháin refers to the groom's ancestry as "De scothaibh Chlanna Míle agus fíor Chonaill cóir". Similarly he calls the Liberator himself "Ó Conaill geal de phór Mhíléisis".

The myth also inspired a large part of a seventeenth-century poem "Tuireamh na hÉireann" or "The Dirge for Ireland" written in about 1650 by Seán Ó Conaill of Caherbarnagh near Loch Currane. According to a genealogical table in "The Last Colonel of the Irish Brigade" the author was a brother of a direct ancestor of the Liberator. The poem retells the story of the invasions. It even identifies a rock in Ballinskelligs Bay on which Éanna, another son of Milesius, perished:

> I gconntae Chiarraí in iarthar Éireann
> de ghlacadar caladh ag Inbhear Sgéine.
> Atá ag bun Choirreáin fós gan traocha
> an charraig ler cailleadh go seachmallach Éanna.

Its main interest, however, is in its bitter account of contemporary events — Cromwellian plantation, dispossession, the suppression of the old Norman and Gaelic families and the executions and transportations that followed.

> Ceann Uí honchubhair ar an spéice
> Transplant, transport go Jamaica
> Dún Gídh, Dún Dágh is Dún Aoinfhir
> gan fhíon, gan cheol, gan dán dá éisteacht.

Cecile O'Rahilly, who edited the poem, notes the words "transport, transplant sound like a knell in the poetry of the period".

The alienation of the native population from the new legal order determines the language of the poem at one point:

> Is docht na dlíthe do rinneadh dár ngéarghoin:
> Siosóin cúirte is téarmaí daora
> wardship livery is Cúirt Exchequer
> cíos coláisde in nomine peonae;
> greenwax, capias, writ, replévin,
> bannaí, fíneáil, díotáil, éigcirt,
> provost, soffré, portré, méara,
> sirriaim, sionascáil, marascáil, chlaona.
> Dlí beag eile do rinneadh do Ghaelaibh,
> surrender ar a gceart do dhéanamh

The litany of legal terms in three languages, all summed up in the word "surrender", has its own pathetic eloquence. It is a litany of alienation, of dispossession. A century and a half later, however, the author's descendant and namesake was to use the language of the law as a statement of repossession.

I loosely translate here a typical passage:

> I mourn the poet Piaras Feiritéar
> whose wine and wit was rich and rare
> until the hangman strangled his elegance
> In Killarney's fairground, a ghastly dance.
> Rebellion's head is high on a stake now
> and warns of pillage and transportation.
> No dún resounds with recitation
> nor wine, nor music, for want of a patron.
> Our leaders are scattered, banished to Connaught
> or soldiers in Spain, forgotten, anonymous.
> Now we have oaths witnessed by their clergy
> the meaningless drivel of landgrabbing perjury.
> Where can we turn, whom can we follow
> now there's no shelter in mountain or forest?
> There's no relief for us from pain
> but to pray to God and his holy saints.

The poem was very well known, occurring in perhaps 200 manuscripts, and at least four different translations into English are known, one published in an 1827 edition. I can't say for certain that Daniel O'Connell knew the poem. If we consider, however, his chosen role as King of the Beggars, it is not unreasonable to suggest that his political base came about from the same sense of dispossession as is expressed in the poem, and that his political power came from his conviction that there was something more to do than simply "pray to God and his holy saints", which was the only relief his ancestor could envisage.

Tomás Rua Ó Súilleabháin was born near Derrynane and lived from 1785 to 1848. He was therefore an acquaintance and a contemporary of Daniel O'Connell who paid for his education as a teacher in Dublin. James Carney has said of the much earlier bardic poets that in composing praise poems for their prince or chief "they had to know Irish genealogy, Irish history and pseudo-history". To some extent Tomás Rua fulfilled this function, albeit in a limited way, in relation to Daniel O'Connell. I have already quoted lines in which he links the O'Connells genealogically with mythological figures. He compares O'Connell to Moses delivering the Israelites from bondage. O'Connell is variously seen as a dragon, a lion, a warrior with bloody sword on high. He is seen as a greater threat to England than Napoleon. Above all, Tomás Rua sees him as someone who will take violent revenge on Protestants and will drive into the ground what he calls "an aicme úd Liútair". Indeed the violence of his language and attitude contrasts highly with the pluralistic constitutionalism of his hero, but as citizens of a state which a century and a half later does not have a pluralistic constitution we should not be surprised that the forces of history worked as they did on Tomás Rua.

In Uíbh Ráthach today Tomás Rua is best remembered for his two great songs "Amhrán na Leabhar" and "Maidin Bhog Álainn i mBá na Scealg". The first of these deals with the "little doom" which Austin Clarke mentioned. Tomás Rua was going to teach in Portmagee and his belongings were being brought by boat from Derrynane Harbour. Just outside the harbour, in calm weather, the boat struck a rock called Carraig Eibhlín Ní Rathaille. Although there was no loss of life Tomás Rua suffered the "little doom" of the loss of all his books. Hence the title of the song, which lovingly names and describes some of his books — history, literature, classics, mathematics, theology, manuscripts and even agricultural textbooks. Its opening lines:

Go cuan Bhéil Inse casadh mé
Cois Goilín aoibhinn Dairbhre
Mar a seoltar flít na farraige
Thar sáile i gcéin

have lifted many a foundering sing-song in Uíbh Ráthach.

His other well-known song "Maidin Bhog Álainn" again deals with boats and sea hazards. This time however he celebrates the deliverance of himself and others after a sudden storm almost capsized their boat on a pilgrimage to Sceilg Michíl or, as he calls it, "carraig glas ard na naomh". Its attractiveness lies in its concrete, specific and evocative descriptions of the storm, rocks, headlands and finally the public house, "tigh Sheáin Mhic Aodha", where they celebrated their escape over a long day and night. Tomás Rua produced no great literature but his work has a special place in Uíbh Ráthach and what might be called his "tíriúlacht" gives a valuable local insight into the larger events of his time.

Finally I would like to turn to a poem which undoubtedly is great literature. Thomas Kinsella has called it "one of the world's great poems". I refer to "Caoineadh Airt Uí Laoire" by Eibhlín Dubh Ní Chonaill, daughter of Máire Ní Dhuibh and aunt of Daniel O'Connell. Máire Ní Dhuibh was related to two families whose names were synonymous in Kerry with Gaelic poetry — the O'Donoghues of the Glens and the family of Piaras Feiritéar whom I mentioned earlier. She herself composed caoineadhs, or laments, as did her aunt Siobhán Ní Dhuibh and another daughter, Alice. Eibhlín Dubh therefore inherited a vibrant tradition. In the depth of her own grief, however, she created something on another plane:

> Mo chara go daingean thú!
> Is cuimhin lem aigne
> An lá breá earraigh úd
> Gur bhreá thíodh hata dhuit
> Faoi bhanda oir tharraingthe,
> Claíomh cinn airgid,
> Lámh dheas chalma,
> Rompsáil bhagarthach -
> Fír-chritheagla
> Ar namhaid chealgach -
> Tú i gcóir chun falaracht
> Is each caol ceanann fút.
> D'úmhlaidís Sasanaigh
> Síos go talamh duit
> Is ní ar mhaithe leat
> Ach le haon-chorp eagla
> Cé gur leo a cailleadh thú
> A mhúirnín mh'anama.

Eibhlín remembers her husband as a heroic warrior, a swashbuckler, silver-hilted sword ready for action and the English bowing low before him. It's no wonder the O'Connells were terrified when Eibhlín laid eyes on him five years earlier. His path was unlikely to accord with the "placid, lotus-eating life of smiling self-realisation" that the O'Connells of Derrynane led in the eighteenth century, according to another O'Connell, I hasten to add. In any event Eibhlín Dubh married without the consent of her family. Their prudence, which was later equally unavailing with Daniel, was well founded. Art was soon an outcast, indeed at times an outlaw, among the landed gentry. Trouble simmered, occasionally boiling over, for some years. Eventually, according to tradition, Abraham Morris, High Sheriff of Cork, offered Art £5 for his valuable horse. The invocation of the archaic Penal Law which required Art, as a Catholic, to sell to Morris, was meant to provoke, and it did. A fight followed and Art was proclaimed again. To make a long story short Art was finally shot dead by a troop of soldiers after he attempted to ambush Morris.

The result was the caoineadh we now have, rooted in the traditions which Eibhlín Dubh had absorbed in Derrynane from which she was now sadly estranged. Eilis Dillon translates:

> My friend you were forever!
> I knew nothing of your murder
> Till your horse came to the stable
> With the reins beneath her trailing
> And your heart's blood on her shoulders
> Staining the tooled saddle
> Where you used to sit and stand.
> My first leap reached the threshold
> My second reached the gateway
> My third leap reached the saddle.
> I struck my hands together
> And I made the bay horse gallop
> As fast as I was able,
> Till I found you dead before me
> Beside a little furze bush
> Without Pope or Bishop
> Without priest or cleric
> To read the death psalms for you,
> But a spent old woman only
> Who spread her cloak to shroud you -
> Your heart's blood was still flowing;
> I did not stay to wipe it
> But filled my hands and drank it.

> Is níor fhanas le hí glanadh
> Ach í ól suas lem bhasaibh.

As Seán Ó Tuama, who edited the poem, points out, these lines, coming on the heels of the pathetic details of her discovery, reach back to the grief of Emer for Cúchulainn and Deirdre for Naoise, who also drank the blood of their dead hero-husbands. Well over a thousand years of tradition inform those last two lines, and yet it is blood we taste, not ritual.

This is because the whole poem is infused not only with stark elemental grief but also with the small everyday details of her grief, the fear of telling her children, the echo of the children's voices through the house in search of their father:

> Mo chara thú go daingean!
> As nuair a thiocfaidh chugam abhaile
> Conchubhar beag an cheana
> Is Fear Ó Laoire, an leanbh,

Fiafróidh díom go tapaidh
Cár fhágas féin a n-athair.
'Neosfad dóibh faoi mhairg
Gur fhágas i gCill na Martar.
Glaofaidh siad ar a n-athair
Is ní bheidh sé acu le freagairt.

Let us jump two centuries forward. In 1985 James Simmons published "Lament for a Dead Policeman" which he puts into the mouth of a woman whose husband, an RUC man, has been murdered. A short extract:

My dearest honey
at our home tonight
what can I answer
Francis and wee Tom
when they ask for Daddy?
I wiped the blood
from our front door
with lukewarm water
and Fairy liquid.
Your gore I swabbed
darling, as you would
have done, my true one.

A very different context — chronologically, socially and politically. Eibhlín Dubh's poem travelled far.

And yet it went further. In 1986 Dermot Bolger published "The Lament for Arthur Cleary". The poem opens as follows:

My lament for you Arthur Cleary
As you lay down that crooked back lane
Under the stern wall of a factory
Where moss and crippled flowers cling

To stone crested by glass and wire
With a runlet of blood over your chest
When I raced screaming towards you
Hearing their cluster of boots retreat

I cupped your face in my palms
To taste life draining from your lips
And you died attempting to smile
As defiant and proud as you had lived.

Behind me I could hear the cry
Of an engine kick-starting to life
And vanishing through laneways
Where we rode on autumn nights.

The horse has become a motorbike and West Cork a Dublin wasteland. Eibhlín Dubh's poem has indeed travelled far.

So let me briefly pull it back two centuries to the southwest. Eibhlín Dubh, while part of what Daniel Corkery categorised as "The Hidden Ireland" or what Thomas Kinsella and Seán Ó Tuama more recently categorised as "The Dispossessed", was no peasant. Coming from an affluent family, well off as landowners and smugglers, she married into another proud affluent household. In Eilis Dillon's translation:

> I never repented it:
> You whitened a parlour for me,
> Painted rooms for me,
> Reddened ovens for me,
> Baked fine bread for me,
> Basted meat for me,
> Slaughtered beasts for me;
> I slept in ducks feathers
> Till midday milking-time
> Or more if it pleased me.

Her own arrogance, the arrogance of her husband and of her class is apparent in the following section, in my own translation:

> My share of the world!
> Bright hilted rider
> Let you rise up now
> Decked out in your finery.
> Put on your high beaver,
> Here are your riding gloves.
> Take up your riding crop
> Your mare is outside waiting.
> Take the eastern by-road,
> With hedges low beside you
> And streams narrow beneath you.
> All heads will bow in greeting
> - If they remember their place
> A thing sadly out of fashion.

And in one of the most moving sections the comfort of wealth and status of which Eibhlín had boasted is invoked, as it were to try to coax her husband home from the "ground sweat" he has taken. John Montague translates:

> My love and my delight!
> Rise up now, straight,
> and come on home with me,
> We'll have a beast slaughtered,
> Call friends to feast,
> Get the music started.

We'll get ready a bed
With crisp linen sheets
And bright speckled quilts
To bring out a sweat instead
Of the chill that grips you.

Art was apparently a noted womaniser, a possible factor in the enmity towards him. When Art's sister, whose hostility towards Eibhlín is a sub-theme of the poem, makes a snide reference, obviously aimed at Eibhlín, to his reputation with women, Eibhlín replies with defiant sexual pride. Thomas Kinsella translates:

My steadfast love!
When you walked through the servile
strong-built towns,
the merchants' wives
would salute to the ground
knowing well in their hearts
a fine bed-mate you were
a great front rider
and father of children

In the next extract, again translated by Thomas Kinsella, Eibhlín seems to anticipate her nephew, Daniel O'Connell, in a resolution which combines perseverance and a faith in the law with a gut feeling which the law is made to serve:

Jesus Christ well knows
there's no cap on my skull
nor shift next my body
nor shoe on my foot-sole
nor stick in my house
nor reins on my brown mare
but I'll spend it on law;
that I'll go across the ocean
to argue with the King,
and if he won't pay attention
that I'll come back again
to the black-blooded savage
that took my treasure.

The imprecation which ends that passage is echoed in the following, translated by Frank O'Connor.

Grief on you, Morris.
Heart's blood and bowel's blood!
May your eyes go blind
and your knees be broken!

This tradition of malevolent cursing was still alive in Kerry in recent times when John B. Keane used it in his play *Sive*.

However, the dominant voice which we hear is the voice of grief and desolation. Thomas Kinsella translates:

> My love and beloved!
> your corn-stacks are standing
> your yellow cows milking.
> Your grief upon my heart
> all Munster couldn't cure
> nor the smiths of Oileán na bhFionn.
> Till Art Ó Laoghaire comes
> my grief will not disperse
> but cram my heart's core,
> shut firmly in
> like a trunk locked up
> when the key is lost.

And, finally, Eibhlín Dubh drags from somewhere the same sense of dignity which Aogán Ó Rathaille summoned in his valedictory poem "Cabhair Ní Ghairfead". The desolate widow, about to enter the graveyard, remembers her social duty. She indeed knows her place. In Thomas Kinsella's translation:

> Women there weeping,
> stay there where you are,
> till Art Mac Conchuir summons drink
> with some extra for the poor
> ere he enter that school
> not for study or for music
> but to bear clay and stones
>
> Ní hag foghlaim léinn na port,
> ach ag iompar cré agus cloch.

The headstrong O'Connell from Derrynane had followed her *gaiscíoch* as far as she could. On her marriage, her brother "The Last Colonel of the Irish Brigade" had written home: "I am sorry to learn that our sister Nelly has taken a step contrary to the will of her parents, but love will not know or hear reason." We may be glad that it did not, because Uíbh Ráthach poetry, and Irish literature as a whole, is far richer for Eibhlín Dubh's imprudent stubbornness.

As I indicated at the beginning I have, most unmethodically, bounced my subject through time and space, through myth and history. My focus has not been academic, nor historical, nor linguistic. What I hope to have shown is the essential contemporaneousness of the widely separated poetry I have dealt with, and thus to establish the resonance of its tradition.

8

O'CONNELL,
MONTALEMBERT AND THE
BIRTH OF CHRISTIAN
DEMOCRACY IN FRANCE

Pierre Joannon

When he reached Paris on 26 March 1847, O'Connell was a dying man, utterly distressed by the tragedy of the Irish Famine, physically as well as mentally diminished by a brain congestion that would take his life less than two months later.

Although helplessly weak, he agreed to receive a delegation of Catholic Liberals led by Count Charles de Montalembert. In a state of utter grief, the Frenchman delivered an address to the pale figure who was lying in a chair, wrapped in a blanket, looking frail and exhausted:

> When I had the great fortune to see you for the first time, sixteen years ago, in your house at Derrynane, on the shores of the Atlantic, we had just gone through the revolution of July, and you were anxiously and ardently preoccupied by the fate of religion in France. I respectfully collected your wishes and your teachings. You then pointed out to us the course we should pursue, and the rules we should follow in order to emancipate the Church from the temporal yoke by legal and civil means, and at the same time to dissociate its cause from all political causes. I have come to present to you the men

who in France have enrolled themselves as the first soldiers under a banner that you were the first to unfurl and that will never disappear. We are all your children or, rather, your pupils. You are our master, our model, our glorious preceptor. It is for that reason we have come to tender you the affectionate and respectful homage we owe to the man of the age who has done most for the dignity and liberty of mankind and especially for the political education of Catholic people.

We are admiring in you the man who has accomplished the most glorious duty that a man can dream of in this world: the man who, without spilling a drop of blood, has reconquered the nationhood of his country and the political rights of eight million Catholics. We have come to salute in you the liberator of Ireland, of that nation which has always evoked brotherly feelings in France and which, thanks to you, will never again fall under the yoke of Protestant fanaticism.

But you are not only the man of a nation, you are the man of the whole of Christendom. Your glory is not Irish only, it is Catholic. Wherever Catholics begin anew to practise civil virtues and devote themselves to the conquest of their civil rights, after God, it is your work. Wherever religion tends to emancipate itself from the thraldom in which several generations of sophists and lawyers have placed it, to you, after God, is religion indebted. May that thought fortify you — revive you in your infirmities, and console you in the afflictions with which your patriotic heart is now overwhelmed. The wishes of Catholic France, of truly Liberal France, will accompany you in your pilgrimage to Rome. The day of your meeting with Pius IX, when the greatest and most illustrious Christian of our age will kneel at the feet of a Pontiff who recalls to our recollection the most brilliant period of our church history, a truly momentous event in the history of our time will take place. If, in that instant of supreme emotion, your heart should entertain a thought not absorbed by Ireland and Rome, remember us! The homage of the affection, respect and devotion of the French people for the Head of the Church could not be better placed than on the lips of the Catholic Liberator of Ireland.

O'Connell was too feeble to make an elaborate answer: "Gentlemen, sickness and emotion close my lips. I should require the eloquence of your president to express to you all my gratitude. But it is impossible for me to utter all I feel. Know, simply, that I regard this demonstration on your part as one of the most significant events of my life."

Significant it certainly was in many respects: it may have reminded O'Connell of his education and early manhood in revolutionary France; it showed him that religion had been eradicated neither by the fire and sword of triumphant Jacobinism nor by the kiss of death of the old dynasty back on the throne after the fall of Napoleon; and last but not least, it gave him the last joy of realising how strong and determining had been the influence of his policies and creed on the emergence of French Catholic Liberalism.

During the French Restoration, which lasted fifteen years, from

Waterloo to the "three glorious days" of the Revolution of July 1830, Catholicism and royalism had been walking hand in hand. The unity of throne and altar which had existed prior to the Great Revolution of 1789 had been re-established by the late Bourbons and had become particularly aggressive and unpopular under the reign of the reactionary mystic Charles X. So much so that all heads of opposition, from the liberal Orleanists to the more extreme Republicans and Bonapartists, were united by anti-religious feelings and beliefs ranging from traditional gallicanism to sarcastic voltairianism and militant atheism and, even more so, by a violent anti-clericalism against the so-called "parti-prêtre", the Congregation and the Jesuit order accused of being the inspirers of the anti-liberal policy of the Court and the State.

The Revolution of July 1830 was directed as much against the throne as against the altar. The fall of the Bourbons was also a defeat for the Church. The mob not only seized the Tuileries, symbol of the monarchy, but also sacked the vestry of Notre Dame, destroyed the calvary of the Mont Valérien, invaded mission houses and seminaries, knocked down crosses and pelted priests and members of religious orders with stones.

This was not just a moment's excess in the heat of a short-lived revolution. It lasted for months after the proclamation of Louis Philippe and the constitution of a Cabinet which could not or did not want to interfere. Churches were closed, others were sacked like Saint Germain l'Auxerrois as late as February 1831, processions were attacked, and ecclesiastical buildings searched allegedly for arms, and for plotters and emissaries of hostile foreign powers. Newspapers and pamphlets were spreading the most obscene stories about the Church and the Catholic faith; bishops and priests were not only denounced as being dissolute and corrupt, but they were also accused of conspiring to bring about a St Bartholomew's massacre against the patriots. Numerous plays written in the same vein were staged to the utter delight of the voltairian bourgeoisie which was to become the backbone of the regime of Louis Philippe. "The Church is in a state of civil death," wrote a contemporary observer. Another remarked: "Some months ago, priests were everywhere: today God is nowhere."

Montalembert himself lamented: "Never was there a nation so officially irreligious." An influential writer, Jules Janin, summed up the situation by saying: "Since the great upheaval of 1789, Catholicism has been mortally sick: the Revolution of July has killed it for good." We find the same obituary under the pen of the German poet Henrich Heine: "The old religion is completely dead; it is already in a state of utter decomposition; the majority of French people do not want to hear any more about this corpse and hold their handkerchief in front of their nose when the Church is mentioned."

From the ruins of the old faith sprang up extravagant new religions like the Eglise Française of the Abbé Châtel, and eccentric social utopias engineered by men like Fourier, Buchez and Saint-Simon, but also a democratic reaction of Catholic clerics and laymen, regenerated by the ordeal, in tune with the new world and dedicated to the total separation of church and state and the lasting reconciliation of religion and freedom. They expressed themselves in *L'Avenir*, the first issue of which was published on 15 October 1830, less than three months after the Revolution of July. At a time when Catholicism did not seem to have any future at all and when believers were more inclined to take refuge in the past than to question the future, *L'Avenir* — *The Future* — was a rather challenging and provocative title for a daily religious newspaper.

Even more provocative was its founder, the Abbé Félicité de Lamennais, possibly the most famous priest in France at the time. A devout Catholic, friend of Chateaubriand, Joseph de Maistre and Bonald, he was at first a staunch traditionalist and a firm believer in the union of throne and altar. Turning his back on what Yeats called "the filthy modern tide", this arch-enemy of the "philosophes" advocated a form of theocracy in which the absolute power of the Christian monarch inspired and guided by the Church would only be limited by the pre-eminence of the Pope. His ultramontanism, so repugnant to French gallican bishops, and the burning intensity of his faith attracted the attention of Rome where Pope Leo XII is believed to have had the intention of making Lamennais a cardinal, partly in gratitude for his strongly worded defence of the faith and the Holy See and partly to cool down his exaltation which often embarrassed Church officialdom.

There was even more embarrassment to come. That was because Lamennais was really more concerned with the altar than with the throne. Enthralled by the awakening of Catholic Ireland under the leadership of O'Connell and disappointed by the Bourbons, who did not think much of his ideas and occasionally censored his writings, the new Bossuet was transformed into a kind of Catholic Rousseau. His switch of allegiance from the King to the People was publicised in his essay, *Progrès de la Révolution et de la guerre contre l'Eglise*, published in 1828. He was still very much enamoured of theocracy, but the People instead of the King was to be the mediator. He strongly advocated public liberties. The Church was fiercely attacked for having spared no effort to identify the cause of religion with the defence of the crown. Lamennais urged the clergy to dissociate themselves from a discredited monarchy, to embrace the cause of democracy and liberalism, and to bless the coming revolution seen as the necessary and providential step towards a new organisation of society which would see the final triumph of the Church. The Revolution of July, which confirmed all his predictions, found Lamennais more convinced than ever of the need to liberalise Catholicism and catholicise liberalism. This is indeed reflected in the defiant epigraph of *L'Avenir*: "Dieu et Liberté" (God and Freedom).

From the start, Lamennais was joined by two men of great energy and talent. The first was Henri Lacordaire, aged twenty-eight, a convert, a scholar and a superb Dominican preacher, burning with love for the holy trinity of faith, freedom and fatherland. The historian Paul Thureau-Dangin writes that Lacordaire saw at once in Lamennais "the O'Connell of French Catholics". Lamennais's second companion was Charles de Montalembert, a young man of twenty, energetic, generous and romantic. Born in Britain of an English mother married to a French aristocrat, member of the Chambre des Pairs during the "Restauration", he had travelled extensively. When he joined the editorial board of *L'Avenir*, he was just back from Ireland where he had met Daniel O'Connell. And from then on, Montalembert would be the link between Ireland and Catholic Liberals in France, who would rely on him to know what was taking place in and outside Dublin, the lessons and examples to be learnt and followed accordingly. Not surprisingly, he would be, in his turn, hailed as "the O'Connell of France".

In fact, so great was Montalembert's role in drawing the attention of his Liberal associates to the Irish question, and pointing out its relevance to the state of French affairs, that it is essential to study his association with Ireland in general and with O'Connell in particular to understand how the influence of the latter was able to shape the very beginning of Christian Democracy in France.

Montalembert had Irish blood in his veins: his maternal grandfather, James Forbes, who had been a decisive influence on his childhood, was related to the Earls of Granard of Castle Forbes, Co. Longford. He gave the speeches of Grattan and Burke to read to his grandson who would be able, years afterwards, to recite them to his schoolmates at Sainte-Barbe. The young Charles de Montalembert later on fell under the influence of a brilliant and forceful Irish churchman, Father MacCarthy, a priest at the Missions Étrangères, who eventually succeeded in converting his Protestant English mother to Catholicism. He was thus prepared to respond enthusiastically to the great patriotic and religious campaign for Emancipation that was taking place in Ireland. In a letter dated 30 November 1828, Montalembert wrote to his friend Léon Cornudet:

> I have decided to write a history of Ireland since 1688, as quickly as possible so that it may be published before the vital question of emancipation is settled.... In achieving this project, I will be eager to pursue two aims: on the one hand I will present France with constitutional models and the example of a nation that lost her freedom through too complacent an attitude towards the throne; on

the other hand I will do justice to Catholicism by describing vividly its virtues and above all the patriotism that it has produced in Ireland.

He asked for books and novels on Ireland, wrote to Grattan's son for information, decided to visit Ireland to study at close range the country and the people, mentioned his "adorable project" to Chateaubriand, and began taking notes in abundance. This frenzy of enthusiasm is attested by several notebooks full of details on Ireland kept in the "Archives Montalembert" at the family estate of La Roche en Brenil.

However, the immaturity of youth — he was barely eighteen — the enormity of the work to be achieved, the sudden realisation of the complexity of the history of Ireland and, above all, the cruel death of his sister, led him to abandon his "adorable project". Bitterly disappointed, he wrote to his friend Cornudet in June 1829: "I had concentrated my life on Ireland, I had identified myself with its past; my heart beat only for her; I practically had only her emotions and interests at heart. It now seems to be that I have lost a beloved friend."

Not entirely, however: Montalembert still devoted a lot of his time to Ireland. In June 1830, he wrote for the *Correspondant* a passionate article on this "country of wonders" where "religion, freedom and poetry inter-twine better than in any other land". Indeed, whether he was dealing with Ireland, the faith and fate of the Church, or the sacred cause of freedom, Montalembert was and would remain all his life a dedicated romantic for whom intuition, imagination and emotion counted far more than abstract reasoning or the sober examination of facts.

He welcomed the fall of the Bourbons because they were old-fashioned, dull and suspicious of freedom and everything he loved and craved for; and because he had convinced himself that the union of the throne and the altar had paralysed the Church and alienated from religion the youth and the people of France. By contrast, the situation in Ireland where O'Connell had united the people of the Church in a formidable non-violent campaign for freedom which had extracted the emancipation of all Catholics in the British Isles from a reticent state, appealed strongly to his imagination eager for heroic action and to his intelligence convinced of the necessity to achieve a total separation between church and state.

It was in this exalted frame of mind that Charles de Montalembert crossed the Irish Channel at long last and set foot in the country of his dreams, at the beginning of September 1830. "I am in a state of continuous enchantment," he wrote to Cornudet. He described his heart "as full of admiration and love for this dear Ireland". More than his own country, he added, Ireland "gratifies all my beliefs, all my tastes, and even the slightest of my prejudices". His exhilaration, which he himself compared to the overwhelming emotion of a pilgrim discovering the Holy Land, is reflected in his unpublished travel diary, in his letters to his close friend Cornudet and, finally, in his famous "Lettre sur le Catholicisme en Irlande", published in January 1831 in *L'Avenir*.

Funnily enough, the only disappointment of his idyllic journey occurred when Montalembert met Daniel O'Connell. The twenty-year-old French aristocrat, full of romantic ideas about Ireland, "this living remnant of the Middle Ages", probably expected to meet in O'Connell a knight in shining armour. But the King of the Beggars was not Arthur in Camelot. When Charles de Montalembert arrived at Derrynane, the door was besieged by one hundred and fifty peasants eager to submit their disputes to the Counsellor. He was brought in by O'Connell himself who displayed a great affability but left him alone in a drawing room overcrowded by a family of biblical proportions! During the dinner the two men were able to talk at great length: "Our conversation", wrote Montalembert, "was essentially devoted to the destinies of France and Catholicism. He confirmed to me the opinions expressed in his admirable letter to the Dublin meeting."

The Dublin meeting in question had been organised by O'Connell's son-in-law, Christopher Fitz-Simon, and financial agent, P.V. Fitzpatrick, to celebrate the Paris Revolution of July. Unable to attend, O'Connell had sent a public letter rejoicing over the event and anticipating, erroneously as it happened, the complete separation of church and state. Because it is an important treatment of the situation in France as well as a major exposition of O'Connell's unorthodox views on religious freedom, and one which would have a determining influence on Montalembert and his associates, it is worth quoting the Liberator at some length:

> The French Revolution is in all its aspects consolatory and deserving of the highest praise...There is one feature in this great and satisfactory change which I hail with the most profound conviction of utility — the complete severance of the church from the state. Infidelity...which had deluged France with the blood of the Catholic clergy, was losing ground by degrees since the concordat obtained by Napoleon; but the progress of Christian truth and genuine piety was much impeded since the return of the Bourbons by the unhallowed commixture of zeal for religion with servile attachment to the Bourbons....The Catholic clergy of France are learned, pious, exemplary and most charitable and zealous. But they were placed in a false position. The events of the first revolution, written in characters of blood, convinced them that the safety of religion was connected with the security of the throne....I heartily rejoice that the last revolution has altered the position....Religion has regained its natural station.

Montalembert was thrilled by the message, but rather put out by the messenger. The next day, after another conversation with the Liberator, he confided to his diary: "He is not a great man altogether, but he is enthusiastic and sensitive and that is already good enough." Later on, in Killarney, he attended a banquet: "O'Connell has spoken, and I am sorry to confess that I have been very disappointed: his language is brusque, pompous, vulgar, his manners unpleasant, his ideas worn out and not connected at all; the only good thing is his voice." With Cornudet he is even more outspoken: "He is only a demagogue; he is by no means a great speaker", and in his diary he concludes sharply: "The more I think about O'Connell, the more I am confirmed in my first impression that he is not a genius or a great man." Years later, however, Montalembert would scribble in the margin of this intemperate youthful utterance: "Oh! What a fool!"

After seven weeks in Ireland, and unable to restrain his enthusiasm, Montalembert confessed: "I am not the same man anymore.... My faith and my earnest attachment to Catholicism are completely changed. I have drawn here ten years of strength and life." Back in Paris, he submitted a long article on Ireland to Lamennais who readily agreed to publish it in *L'Avenir* out of consideration for the brilliant qualities of thought and style displayed by the author, and out of deep concern for an exemplary situation that had attracted his attention from the outset. Indeed, it is easy to see that Lamennais himself dreamed of emulating "this O'Connell who pushes, with a strong arm, the old world into the abyss and proclaims the reign of a new right, the right of the people, of liberty and equality.... This colossal revolutionary!"

Montalembert's "Lettre sur le Catholicisme en Irlande" was published in three separate issues of *L'Avenir* dated 1, 5 and 18 January 1831. It sang the praises of a popular Church sharing the pains and miseries of the people and, like them, "free, poor and invincible". It marvelled at the "stubborn love of freedom and nationalism" of Catholic priests which explained why, in the face of so many persecutions, the native Irish remained steadfastly faithful to the old religion. It rejoiced in the love of France exhibited by the Irish of every origin and class, and more specifically in the warm sympathy expressed by the Irish bishops for the Revolution of July, a sympathy that Montalembert had already seen at work at the Irish College in Paris. Couched in the most romantic language, Montalembert's eulogy of Ireland was an immediate success. It was widely quoted; issued in pamphlet form; highly praised by Victor Hugo, Sainte-Beuve and Alfred de Vigny; and even translated into German and English (in Ireland, it was published in the *Cork Mercantile Chronicle* of 26 October 1831).

In the spring of 1831, famine having once more broken out in Ireland, Montalembert published a vibrant appeal to the innate sense of charity of French Catholics. A relief committee was set up and a subscription was launched by *L'Avenir*. Local committees were formed in Alsace, Auvergne and Provence. Eighty thousand francs — quite a considerable sum for the time — was eventually collected and sent to Ireland between June and September 1831.

Individually, Montalembert helped many Irish expatriates. His archives are full of letters of thanks and notes about his assistance. He seems to have rendered numerous services to the Irish College in Paris. Furthermore, he was the best propagandist that Ireland could have dreamed of. He lectured Hugo, Vigny, Musset, Michelet and Guizot on Ireland. He gave precious indications to Alexis de Tocqueville and Gustave de Beaumont, prior to their famous Irish journey of 1835. He strongly influenced Frédéric Ozanam, founder of the Society of Saint Vincent de Paul, who wrote a couple of interesting essays on Ireland in his *Etudes Germaniques* and eventually became an ardent republican. And it is not hazardous to suggest that he was probably influential in shaping the ideas expressed by Lacordaire in his brilliant funeral oration on O'Connell, pronounced at Notre Dame on 10 February 1848.

Ireland and O'Connell never ceased to occupy the mind and the heart of Montalembert. *Moines d'Occident*, his last work, published in seven volumes between 1860 and 1867, vividly recalled "the shining cradle of Ireland" and the time when the "Island of Saints" was sending legions of scholars and monks to teach and evangelise the continent. At the very end of his life, he would again express his sadness at not having been able to write the history of this "modern Palestine", "a splendid history that has not found yet a historian worthy of it".

He also paid numerous tributes to the Liberator in various essays like *Des Intérêts Catholiques au XIXe siècle* (1852) or *De l'Avenir Politique de l'Angleterre* (1856), showing that he had overcome the arrogant severity of his youth. Indeed, he honoured the memory of O'Connell "with the immortal glory of having liberated his religion and given a new life to his country by the sole means of legal action, without having spilled a single drop of blood in the process".

The Liberator of Ireland and the leader of the French Catholic Liberals shared the same open and generous conception of civil and religious freedom. They also clung to the belief that Catholics had an inalienable right to receive a Catholic education in schools, colleges and universities placed under ecclesiastical control. This basic freedom was denied to French Catholics, even though Catholic institutions for girls were tolerated. In 1831, Montalembert, Lacordaire, de Coux and their associates launched a vigorous campaign which roused a great deal of enthusiasm in public opinion and made it impossible for the government to preserve the system of disqualification set up by Napoleon: the freedom of primary education was recognised by an Act dated 28 June 1833. The ensuing campaign to obtain the freedom of secondary education was fiercely resisted by the political establishment and only faintly supported by the French hierarchy. All the same, it was at last granted in 1850 by the famous "Loi Falloux" which is still part of the law of the land today. On many occasions during these stormy campaigns, Montalembert referred to Ireland, quoting the Liberator and praising the achievement by peaceful means of religious freedom and "political equality of Catholics and Protestants within the vast British Empire".

Montalembert not only shared most of O'Connell's ideas, he was also inspired by his methods. In November 1830, he professed to have already in mind "a Catholic Association founded on the same principles as the Catholic Association of Ireland". The Agence Générale pour la Défense de la Liberté Religieuse, founded one month later, was indeed modelled on the Catholic Association of O'Connell. And so was the Comité Central Catholique launched by Montalembert in 1844. Unlike O'Connell, however, Montalembert failed to mobilise the Church: the bishops who had no intention whatsoever of antagonising the government flatly refused his call to lead the Committee. *L'Oeuvre du denier de Saint Pierre*, also initiated by Montalembert, was similarly inspired by O'Connell's Catholic rent — a small weekly contribution of one penny levied from Catholics in every parish of Ireland.

The difference between the father of modern Irish democracy, as Seán Ó Faoláin calls the Liberator, and the founders of the Catholic Liberal tradition in France resides essentially in the attitude of the Church. In Ireland, the Church was carried away by O'Connell who resorted to persuasiveness and flexibility to cement the unfailing support of the clergy and the Catholic masses. Whether willingly or reluctantly, Rome had to follow. In France, the picture was very different. Lamennais showed himself difficult and unflinching. He antagonised a wide section of the clergy which still adhered to gallicanism, irritated conservative Catholics who could not envisage a church separated from the throne, failed to mobilise the masses in the country and, finally, lost whatever support and sympathy he had in Rome. The encyclical *Mirari Vos* having emphatically condemned his "errors", Lamennais broke away from the Church and was abandoned by his former friends, Montalembert and Lacordaire, who remained faithful to the Holy See as "penitent Catholics and impenitent Liberals". The *Syllabus*, coming after *Mirari Vos*, would further distress those defeated Liberals who still dreamt of the fusion of Catholicism and democracy.

Professor Maurice O'Connell has an interesting theory to explain why O'Connell succeeded where Lamennais, Montalembert and Lacordaire failed:

That O'Connell should have escaped censure by Rome for his unorthodox views is easily explained. He lived in the English-speaking Protestant world where Catholicism had little to lose and much to gain from religious freedom and separation of church and state. Furthermore he was a layman, and Rome was more tolerant of heterodoxy in laity than in clergy. His enormous popularity in Ireland and his normally friendly relations with the Irish clergy were additional reasons why Rome would hesitate to confront him. Unlike the French Liberal Catholics, who imprudently appealed to Gregory XVI for a judgement on their principles, O'Connell avoided theological debates in this context. He was careful to express his views in a political rather than a theological frame.

However, the seed of Catholic Liberalism had been sown on French soil. New sowers would follow like Ozanam, Armand de Melun, Albert de Mun and many others. Endless crops would flourish and give birth to numerous periodicals acting as centres of Christian Democrat influence like the *Sillon* of Marc Sangnier, *Ouest Eclair* of Emmanuel Desgrès du Lou and Father Trochu, *La Quinzaine* of Georges Fonsegrive, *Les Semaines Sociales* of Marius Gonin, *L'Aube* of Francisque Gay, and others; and even to political parties reminiscent of Montalembert's Committee and O'Connell's Association, more in their aims than in their achievements which were always limited, like the Parti Démocrate Populaire of 1924, the Nouvelles Equipes Françaises of 1938 and the postwar Mouvement Républicain Populaire (MRP) which participated in nearly every government of the Fourth Republic.

Ireland remained a source of inspiration to some of the leaders of this political persuasion. Indeed, it must be remembered that Marc Sangnier, who was a strong supporter of Ireland's War of Independence, delivered a strongly worded lecture on 28 June 1920, entitled "Pour l'Irlande Libre", at the end of which he referred explicitly to Montalembert's deep love for Ireland and quoted at great length the funeral oration on O'Connell by Lacordaire; and it is to be recorded that Francisque Gay wrote a passionate study on *L'Irlande et la Société des Nations* published in 1921.

But the last leader of public opinion in France who may have been inspired by O'Connell was not a Christian Democrat, even if he was a sincere Christian and a true democrat. He was former president Charles de Gaulle. His maternal grandmother had published a life of the Liberator which was to be one of the earliest books to be read by the general. One of his biographers, David Schoenbrun, does not hesitate to suggest that "What influenced him most was a romantic narrative, *The Liberator of Ireland or Life of Daniel O'Connell.* He would always remember this inspiring example of resistance to religious and national persecution." One is tempted to lend credence to it when one sees de Gaulle, in the evening of his life, visiting O'Connell's house in Derrynane and amazing those close to him with his detailed knowledge of Irish history in general and of the life of this great champion of people's rights in particular, as recalled by Admiral Flohic, his ADC who escorted him in Ireland in 1969.

9

O'CONNELL AND GERMAN POLITICS

Peter Alter

Daniel O'Connell was one of the most famous contemporary figures of the 1830s and 1840s in Europe, as he was in Germany. He was named in the same breath as such enlightened spirits as the Frenchmen Lafayette and Lamennais. The Rhenish democrat, writer and journalist Jakob Venedey, who had long been the London correspondent for several German newspapers and had himself visited Ireland, in 1840 called O'Connell one of the "greatest, most powerful political characters" in the history of the world.[1] In a popular German encyclopaedia published in 1848, the same Venedey called O'Connell "the greatest Irishman of all times, the great man of the century".[2] The well-known south-German Liberal Carl von Rotteck had pictures of Lafayette and O'Connell hanging above his desk. During the 1830s and 1840s many books and pamphlets about the life and politics of O'Connell were published in Germany, informing their readers about political and economic conditions in Ireland. They had titles such as: *Ireland and O'Connell. Contribution to an understanding of the recent history of Ireland. Together with O'Connell's trial, at the same time continuing an examination of ancient and modern conditions in Ireland; Daniel O'Connell, his life and work; Ireland and the repeal issue. A few words about O'Connell's campaign for the repeal of the union between Great Britain and Ireland; and O'Connell and his trial.*[3]

In 1838, twenty-three-year-old Otto von Bismarck, later to become Germany's first Imperial Chancellor, named O'Connell, as well as Robert Peel and Mirabeau, as the models he wanted to emulate. For Bismarck's level of intellectual and political development at the time, the letter to his father of September 1838 in which he made this statement is a precocious document. "I must admit", he wrote, "that I am not free of this passion (to command, to be admired and famous) and the honour accorded, for example, to a soldier at war, to a statesman under a free constitution, like Peel, O'Connell, Mirabeau, i.e. someone who participates in vigorous political movements, attracts me to the exclusion of all other considerations, like a moth to the light."[4] When the Prussian politician Ernst Ludwig von Gerlach travelled to Britain and Ireland in the summer of 1844, the Prussian king, Frederick William IV, summoned him to an audience in Potsdam before he left. The king dismissed von Gerlach by asking him to convey his greetings to O'Connell.[5] Von Gerlach did in fact visit O'Connell in prison and described the rather disappointing meeting in his diary.[6]

This extraordinarily strong interest in O'Connell and Ireland was a totally new phenomenon in the Germany of the 1830s and 1840s. Until the mid-1820s, the general public in Germany had shown little interest in Ireland, for them a remote island in the Atlantic Ocean, halfway between England and America. It was rare to find anyone with detailed knowledge of Ireland's political, economic and social problems, or of the island at all. At most, a few philologists and literary scholars were interested in the Emerald Isle, especially in the second half of the eighteenth century, during the Ossianic revival.[7] Not even Edmund Burke's criticism of England's Irish policy and his defence of the Irish Catholics (for example, in his *Letter to Sir Hercules Langrishe*) aroused much interest in Germany, despite the great influence which Burke's political theory had on German political thinking from the late eighteenth century onwards.[8]

Here is only one example — but an interesting one — of the general ignorance of conditions in Ireland which was fairly typical of Germany until about 1830. On 7 April 1829, eighty-year-old Johann Wolfgang von Goethe, the most famous contemporary German writer and a statesman as well as a scholar, was talking about Ireland with a friend. Johann Peter Eckermann, Goethe's companion and secretary, gave this report of the conversation:

> As I entered, I found Hofrath Meyer...sitting with Goethe at table.... They spoke of art — of Peel, who has given four thousand pounds for a Claude Lorrain, and has thus found especial favour in the eyes of Meyer.
> The newspapers were brought in, and we looked over them while waiting for the soup. The emancipation of the Irish was now discussed.

> "It is instructive", said Goethe, "to see how things of which nobody ever thought and which would never have been spoken of but for the present crisis come to light on this occasion. Though we cannot get a clear notion of the state of Ireland (the subject is too intricate), this we can see: she suffers from the evils that will not be removed by any means — not by emancipation. If it has hitherto been unfortunate for Ireland to endure her evils alone, it is now unfortunate that England is also drawn into them. Then, no confidence can be put in the Catholics. We see with what difficulty the two million Protestants in Ireland have kept their ground hitherto against the preponderating five million Catholics; how for instance the poor Protestant farmers have been oppressed, tricked and tormented, when among Catholic neighbours. The Catholics do not agree among themselves, but they always unite against a Protestant. They are like a pack of hounds; which bite one another, but, when a stag comes in view, all unite immediately to run it down."

Then, Eckermann notes: "From Ireland conversation turned to the affairs of Turkey."[9]

Goethe's comments on Ireland, made in April 1829, are also illuminating because they reflect the German educated public's growing interest in Ireland as well as its prejudices. In the late 1820s Ireland came to the attention of the educated public in Germany almost overnight — undoubtedly as the result of O'Connell's work, his vigorous and well-publicised agitation for Catholic Emancipation, and later for the Repeal of the Union. As far as the Germans were concerned, one could safely say that O'Connell put Ireland on the map.

One more example may illustrate this sudden change in perception. In 1844 a pamphlet by an anonymous author was published under the sensational title *England versus O'Connell, or the world trial*. In an introductory section headed "Whence the sympathy", the author explained why Germany and the whole of Europe were gripped by compassion for O'Connell and Ireland. The first reason put forward by the author was the remarkable fact that O'Connell sacrificed himself, exposed himself to danger and took on the British government purely out of love for his people. This, the author pointed out with heavy irony, distinguished him from other contemporary "democrats and demagogues". Interest in O'Connell and Ireland was strengthened, the author continued, by the gradually increasing popularity of constitutional ideas. Another factor, the author suggests, is the hatred which German merchants felt for England, which grew out of professional jealousy, and embraced enthusiasm for Ireland. It gradually had communicated itself to the whole of the German population.[10]

Finally, this anonymous author writes that the Catholic Church had contributed to the pro-Irish atmosphere in Germany. It is true that, since the mid-1820s, the echo of the agitation for Catholic Emancipation had reached as far as Germany. Goethe's remarks are a telling illustration of this. The campaign stimulated interest in Ireland and its problems, especially as the rapid improvement in communications allowed more information, and more reliable information, to flow from Ireland. German travellers visiting England now more frequently than ever before went over to Ireland as well, and tried to gain a picture of the country by seeing it on the spot (and their interest was not always purely political, but covered a wide range of subjects). One of the first to report from O'Connell's Ireland on the basis of personal impressions was the Silesian prince Hermann von Pückler-Muskau who knew O'Connell personally. His description of Irish conditions in 1828 and 1829 was so well thought of that, in the following years, Pückler-Muskau was constantly cited in Germany as an authority on Ireland — along with the later, similarly unpolitical traveller, Johann Georg Köhl, who in 1842 and 1843 witnessed the Ireland of the Repeal period.[11] Following the great expansion of the political press around 1830, however, the main source informing the German public about Ireland was newspapers. At first, they only published extracts from English papers, but then, as their network of correspondents grew, they also printed eye-witness accounts.

Germany soon went beyond merely registering conditions in Ireland, and a fundamental public discussion of the Irish question and its many facets ensued. At O'Connell's time, political events in Ireland seemed to be assuming a European dimension in the eyes of the Germans. It became apparent to what extent Ireland was endangering the stability and unity of the United Kingdom, at that time the richest and most powerful state in the world. Further, these events raised the more general question of the revolutionary nature of the widespread agitation in Ireland, and of O'Connell's role, in Ireland as well as in Europe, as the champion of freedom, equality and justice. Thus the Irish question and, in particular, the politician O'Connell, moved into the centre of the sometimes acrimonious political debate between German conservatives and liberals in the years leading up to the revolutions of 1848-49. By the 1830s and 1840s, O'Connell had in fact become a controversial figure in German politics. He inspired enthusiasm, affection and veneration — but his name also engendered disapproval, protest and even hatred.

For the vast majority of Catholics in Germany and for the often persecuted supporters of the liberal and national movement, O'Connell was a hero and a model to be copied. Both groups, the Catholics and the liberal nationalists, claimed O'Connell for themselves. For the German Catholics O'Connell was naturally, in the first instance, the man of Catholic Emancipation, the "Liberator" who had fought gallantly for the freedom of the Catholic Church in Ireland and its followers. For the German liberals and supporters of the growing national movement, O'Connell was primarily an uncompromising opponent of national and political oppression, a man who had tried to lead the Irish people out of political tutelage and dependence by peaceful means. At the same time, the liberal nationalists saw O'Connell as the embodiment of a modern liberal Catholic, a type of politician with whom they could combine in future struggles. Consequently, between 1830 and 1848 in Germany, O'Connell's name evoked associations with German problems, aspirations and objectives. His activities in Ireland made Germans with political interests reflect upon the state and the nation in their own country, upon revolution and freedom in their universal meaning. O'Connell's policies provided arguments for liberals, Catholics, and conservatives in pursuit of their own goals.[12]

German liberals, who were calling for a unified Germany with a democratic constitution, were naturally very sympathetic towards Irish demands for religious and political freedom, Ireland's "holy cause", as a south German journalist put it.[13] They constantly emphasised parallels with their own miserable position under the authoritarian yoke of Metternich, and felt strongly there was a connection with their own ideas and ideals. Their admiration for O'Connell, as indicated earlier, reached a peak in the early 1840s. The politician journalist Ludwig Wittig wrote a poem in 1844 entitled "The Harpist" ("Der Harfner") which was published in *Vorwärts! Volkstaschenbuch auf das Jahr 1845* whose editor was Robert Blum,[14] the well-known liberal, later executed by order of a court martial during the 1848 revolution in Vienna. Wittig wrote in a somewhat awkward rhyme scheme: "The harpist is an old man, / But his eye still flashes brightly; / If you don't recognize him as King Dan, / Then call him O'Connell. / Green Erin in his harp, / and masterly his playing, / Right through the dense ranks of the loyal / His song resounds: 'Repeal!'" And now in German:

> Der Harfner ist ein alter Mann,
> Doch blitzt sein Auge hell;
> Kennt ihr ihn nicht als König Dan,
> So nennt ihn O'Connell.
> Grün Erin ist die Harfe sein,
> Und meisterhaft sein Spiel,
> Voll durch der Treuen dichte Reihn
> Erschallt sein Lied : "Repeal!"

The veneration of O'Connell also took other forms. In 1843, for example, the classified section of the widely-read liberal *Kölnische Zeitung* carried an advertisement offering for sale "well-captured portraits" of O'Connell.[15]

If one looks beyond this sort of effusive enthusiasm for O'Connell, however, closer inspection reveals a range of nuances among the reactions of German liberals. While some unconditionally supported O'Connell's activities, others had much greater reservations about these events. The latter were those liberals who took English liberalism and the English constitution as a model which they would not question under any circumstance. They were dedicated Anglophiles, such as the historian Friedrich Christoph Dahlmann, who showed little understanding for conditions in Ireland. He, in 1835 (like Goethe six years earlier), lamented the fact that "England today" is suffering "above all from the Irish question". But at the same time Dahlmann did not despair and emphasised that "England's constitution" had "never been more purified". England's strength was not in doubt.[16]

Yet other liberals who believed earnestly in the ideas of the French Revolution and French political thinking did not share this sort of uncritical admiration for England and its constitution. On the contrary, their pro-Irish feelings were connected with vehement criticism of political abuses and aberrations in the United Kingdom. Carl von Rotteck exemplifies this attitude. Writing in 1831 he referred to the "illiberal restrictions" under which Catholics in Ireland still suffered. He claimed that the "upheaval which daily threatens in Ireland" was by no means a consequence of O'Connell's agitation, but the result of English repressive policies. Rotteck described the union of Ireland and Great Britain as "unnatural" and called for its unconditional repeal as the "civil emancipation" of the Irish which reason demanded.[17]

Liberal sympathy for Ireland and O'Connell even swelled into a mass movement where liberals found themselves in one camp with democrats and Catholics in areas of central Europe where they had common interests and shared the struggle against despotism and governmental oppression. This was the case above all in the Catholic Rhineland which, since the Congress of Vienna, had belonged to the kingdom of Prussia, a state with a majority of Protestants. In the Rhineland and, to a lesser extent, in neighbouring Westphalia the parallel with the Irish struggle for religious and civil freedom could most easily be drawn. Therefore, there are numerous examples of Rhenish adulation of O'Connell. Two illustrations should suffice. The "Open Letter from Germany to O'Connell", dated March 1844 and penned by a liberal lawyer from Bonn, finished thus: "The whole of Germany, the whole of Europe, has its eyes fixed upon you and your island. You will prove to be worthy of the great task which God has placed upon your shoulders."[18] O'Connell's release from prison, the second example, prompted the citizens of Koblenz and its surrounding area to organise a big demonstration and salute him as a "great martyr for the religious and civil rights of his people, the glorious liberator, the best citizen of all times". In addition and to give their admiration more

115

substance, the people of Koblenz donated a barrel "of the best Rhenish wine" as a gift for O'Connell.[19] Unfortunately there is no evidence as to whether the barrel ever reached him.

The Catholics in the Prussian Rhineland after 1815 certainly did not see themselves as "Prussia's Irish"; nor can there be any question of demands for autonomy along the lines of Repeal. This shows that the political struggle in the Rhineland was much less bitter than that in Ireland. The social and national antagonisms which were such essential ingredients in the conflict in Ireland were missing. Nevertheless, the Prussian government in Berlin observed the co-operation between Catholics, democrats, and liberals in the Rhineland and other parts of Prussia with great suspicion and even alarm.

In the late 1830s, the Prussian government registered with much anxiety and nervousness signs that a Catholic party was forming on a democratic basis. A memorandum by the Prussian administration in the Rhineland, dated 23 February 1838, pointed to the political significance of the fact that O'Connell had several times received information "about the condition of Catholicism on the Rhine".[20] Irish-German links must, therefore, have existed at that time, although unfortunately we know no more about them. An anonymous letter from Paris, posted at about the same time, similarly alerted the Prussian government to O'Connell's influence on German Catholics, and to the fact that O'Connell's friend Waterton had travelled through the Rhineland.[21] In 1840 the allegation that a prominent Protestant liberal, David Hansemann, had compared himself to O'Connell, was enough to make the president of the administrative district of Aachen suspect him of "aspiring to be the head and leader of a political party".[22] Political parties were banned at that time in Prussia and other parts of Germany. The mention of O'Connell's name alone was enough to conjure up visions of effective opposition or even threats to the existing state among both people and governments. Among the majority of the people, O'Connell's name evoked acclamation; among the governments, unease and occasionally exaggerated reactions. For example, when eighty Catholic priests in the southern German kingdom of Württemberg collected among their flocks £85 for the cause of Repeal in 1844, the police were swift to confiscate the money and the priests were prosecuted.[23]

The reactions of conservative German politicians and journalists to O'Connell and the problems of Ireland were in line with those of the various governments in power. German conservatives feared and rejected O'Connell. They condemned his objectives as revolutionary and felt the same unease about this agitation as they did about the co-operation between Catholics and liberals in Belgium. For example, in the autumn of 1839 a well-known conservative journalist, Karl Ernst Jarcke, who had worked for many years in Metternich's chancellery in Vienna, noted with concern that "the highly dangerous example of Ireland and O'Connell" might set a precedent in Germany and the entire Catholic world. Jarcke feared the "oppositional movement in Ireland", and the spectre of nationalism which he believed was lurking behind O'Connell's campaign.[24] Ireland's striving for independence from England, embodied so visibly by O'Connell, was interpreted by the conservatives as part and parcel of the European revolutionary movement which threatened to destroy the established order in state and society. The *Berliner Politisches Wochenblatt*, then one of Germany's leading conservative journals and dedicated to combat "revolution in all its guises", welcomed Catholic Emancipation. In 1835, however, it regretted that Emancipation had opened the door to the House of Commons, and thus to power and influence in British politics, for the liberal and allegedly radical-revolutionary elements in Ireland led by the notorious O'Connell.[25]

The same year, 1835, witnessed the publication in Germany of "An account of the present condition of Ireland". The anonymous author of the pamphlet wrote: "The amalgamation of the Catholics with the Revolution" must not be accepted. He went on: "The radical and revolutionary tendency which is expressed in everything which O'Connell and his followers do, must be condemned in principle." He claimed that O'Connell's agitation caused unrest and upheaval in Ireland, bloody resistance to the power of the state, and ultimately anarchy.[26] Even Catholic supporters of the conservative cause could not be persuaded to soften their attitude towards the Irish movement by pointing to its Catholic character. Their rejection of the "agitator" and "demagogue" O'Connell, his aims and policies, was straightforward and unrelenting. For them he was not a true friend of the Church; his ideas were rooted in the French Revolution.[27]

Further quotations are not necessary. There can be no doubt whatsoever of how much the fascinating figure of O'Connell and the Irish question occupied the minds of the German public in the 1830s and 1840s. O'Connell was drawn into Germany's political debates at the time and, depending on political sympathies, held up as a model for liberals and democrats, or pointed to as an awful example of a revolutionary agitator by conservatives. Catholics and liberal nationalists in Germany attached their own hopes and expectations of improvements in the political situation of their country to O'Connell's successes, which they admired as the result of a policy of non-violence. Conservatives, on the other hand, invoked O'Connell's name in order to support and secure the political and social *status quo* in Prussia and other German states.

With the benefit of hindsight, the historian can make the proposition that constant reference to O'Connell and Ireland and to the astonishing political mobilisation of the Irish population, was undoubtedly a contributory factor in preparing the ground for the revolutions of 1848-49 in central Europe. It will be difficult for the historian, however, to find evidence in the documents which will prove this proposition. I would, therefore, rather leave it here as an open question.

After O'Connell's death and the failure of the central European revolutions, O'Connell's image faded very quickly in Germany. Interest in Ireland diminished generally. Germans did not look towards Ireland again until the beginning of the Land War and the rise of the Home Rule movement a generation later. But then the name of O'Connell was totally overshadowed by that of a new Irish leader.

10

O'CONNELL'S IMPACT ON THE ORGANISATION AND DEVELOPMENT OF GERMAN POLITICAL CATHOLICISM*

Geraldine Grogan

I would like to start with a quotation from the German Catholic newspaper the *Katholische Sonntagsblätter* of 5 September 1848:

> Once again we would like to bring to the attention of our readers the greatest man of the century, the Liberator of Ireland, Daniel O'Connell. This is the man who freed his demoralised people from three hundred years of planned oppression. He is the great apostle of freedom and peace, the conqueror of England.

The purpose of this paper is to demonstrate the role played by O'Connell, as both a symbol and as a working model, for the development and organisation of German political Catholicism between the years 1830 and 1850.

Of particular significance is the impact of his organisational and propaganda policies on key members of the German Catholic intel-

---

* *The Noblest Agitator: Daniel O'Connell and the German Catholic Movement 1830-1850* by Geraldine Grogan is published by Veritas (Dublin, 1991).

ligentsia, on men such as Joseph Görres, Ignaz von Döllinger, Franz Josef Ritter von Buss and Adam Franz Lennig.[1] Following on from this is his importance for the development of the Piusverein für religiöse Freiheit, an organisation established in Mainz in the hectic days of the 1848 revolution and subsequently renamed the Katholischer Verein Deutschlands at the first general assembly of the organisation held in October of that year. This organisation — which survives today as the Katholikentage — was the first formal indication that by the mid-nineteenth century there existed a powerful, determined, united Catholic front in Germany.

By that time the international image of O'Connell was already well established. Throughout America, Australia, Britain and continental Europe, news of his demands for a Church free from secular interference and for the Repeal of the Act of Union aroused considerable interest, of a negative as well as a positive nature. Governments, among them those in Berlin and Vienna, viewed the development of O'Connell's popular mass movements with disquiet, while many of their citizens, in particular the members of the increasingly politically aware Catholic middle classes, saw in O'Connell's campaigns the blueprint for the establishment of their own organisations, which could aid them in their endeavours to achieve improved civil and religious rights for the Catholic Church and its followers. This is especially true in the case of German Catholics, who founded a virtual replica of O'Connell's Catholic Association in March 1848. While branches of this organisation were established in each of the German states, the initial impetus came from three main areas — the Bavarian capital of Munich, which was the home of the so-called Görres Circle, the liberal state of Baden, where Franz Josef Ritter von Buss was active, and the Prussian-controlled Catholic Rhineland. Thus, in examining the impact of O'Connell on Catholic Germany the geographical terms of reference are best set at these three centres of O'Connellite influence.

There are many factors which favoured the progress of O'Connell's ideas in Catholic circles in these areas in the period between the revolutions of 1830 and 1848. Not least in terms of importance was the growing political awareness of German Catholic intellectuals in general and the impact upon them of members of the vibrant French Liberal Catholic movement, which was decidedly pro-O'Connell in its sentiments. The ideas of Charles de Montalembert (1810-70), Félicité de Lamennais (1782-1854) and Henri-Dominique Lacordaire (1802-61) spread among their German co-religionists not merely by means of the publication of most of their works in German translation immediately after their appearance in France and the popularity of their journal *L'Avenir*, but also by the establishment of close personal contacts with influential German Catholics, like Görres and Döllinger. In addition the general

European fascination with the personality of O'Connell, resulting in increased coverage of the political struggles in Ireland in both the popular and the embryonic Catholic press in Germany, as well as in the widely read travelogues on journeys to the "wild" and "romantic" island of Ireland, did much to popularise O'Connell's successful tactics and campaigns. Indeed this awareness of O'Connell's success — particularly in 1829 when he achieved Catholic Emancipation — is a key factor. For while realising the similarities between the Catholics in the Rhineland and those in Ireland (both faced with strong anti-Catholic Protestant administrations) the Rhenish Catholics also saw how their Irish counterparts, under the dynamic leadership of O'Connell, had fought what was perhaps the greatest military power of the era and had won a significant battle for their rights with the achievement of Catholic Emancipation. The entry on O'Connell in Volume IV of the first edition of Herder's Catholic encyclopaedia (*Conversations-Lexikon*), which appeared in 1855, supports this view:

> O. [O'Connell] was the noblest and greatest of all agitators, as the English themselves recognised; he led his oppressed people in a movement to achieve their rights and never once stepped outside the law; he forbade any act of violence or bloodshed and in so doing awoke and nurtured the noble principles of the people. In this way he forced an embittered and powerful enemy to show respect and justice.

O'Connell's determination to avoid violence at all costs and achieve his demands by moral force alone is one of the main aspects of the large amount of coverage of the Irish leader in the Catholic press in Germany at this time. Consequently, the popularity of O'Connell and his campaigns grew, not only among the Catholic intelligentsia, but also among ordinary people, who treated him as a national folk hero; many homes in the Rhineland had portraits of O'Connell on the wall (indeed an advertisement in the popular liberal newspaper the *Allgemeine Zeitung* of 6 October 1844 reminded its readers where such items could be purchased!), addresses of support were sent to him and poems and books written about him and dedicated to him.[2] Indeed, on his release from Richmond Jail in 1844, the citizens of Koblenz celebrated in style, even sending the Liberator a barrel of the finest Rhenish wine! Such popularity was of vital importance in the invocation to O'Connell's policies and personality in the establishment of the Piusverein für religiöse Freiheit in 1848.

Moreover, the circumstances of the German Catholic Church in the first half of the nineteenth century were particularly favourable to the spread of O'Connell's ideas and the development of an organisation based on the structure and tactics of his Catholic Association in the states of the

German Confederation. In the early decades of the nineteenth century the German Catholic Church was virtually under attack. There were first of all the effects of the French Revolution with its ideas of radical democracy and its avowed anticlericalism. Then there were the secularisation policies in the German states, whereby the ecclesiastical estates were carved up by temporal rulers in a development known as "the Princes' Revolution", and the dissolution of the Holy Roman Empire in 1806. Finally came the agreements made at the Congress of Vienna in 1814-15, especially those which placed the Catholic populations of the Rhineland and Belgium respectively under the authority of the Protestant rulers Friedrich Wilhelm III of Prussia and William of Orange of the Netherlands. All these developments produced a Church lacking in self-confidence and a sense of unity. Conversely, however, these changes had a positive effect. With secularisation, the hierarchy gradually became more middle class in outlook and character and the Church was forced to rely on its own resources. This slowly evolved into a movement towards greater spirituality in the Church — led by the Landshut-based Professor of Moral and Pastoral Theology, Johann Michael Sailer (1751-1832) — towards an upsurge in popular piety among Catholics[4] and also towards greater politicisation. Moreover, German Catholics were also encouraged by the revolt of Belgian liberals and Catholics in 1830, which led to the establishment of an independent Belgian state and restored the Church to a position of authority within the state, on friendly terms with the liberal government. Nonetheless, it was not until the controversy aroused by the pamphlet *Athanasius*, written in defence of the Archbishop of Cologne, Clemens August Freiherr von Droste zu Vischering, who was arrested and imprisoned by the Prussian authorities in 1837 (an event known as the Cologne Incident), that German political Catholicism became a real and vibrant force.

The immediate cause of the Cologne Incident was the mixed-marriage issue, but the deeper cause was the Church's opposition to the claims of the state in what had hitherto been the sole responsibility of the Church. In the Rhineland many Prussian officers married local Catholic women. In 1830, despite the Prussian government's opposition to the children of such unions being brought up in the Catholic faith, the Vatican gave permission for Catholic priests to render passive assistance at the marriage of such a couple. Not content with this, the Prussian government in June 1834 made a secret agreement with the then Archbishop of Cologne, von Spiegel, and with a number of other bishops, whereby Catholic priests would solemnly consecrate such marriages. Following von Spiegel's death in August 1835, Droste zu Vischering became Archbishop of Cologne. Upon discovering the secret dealings with the authorities, he decided to ignore them and returned to the 1830 ruling of the Vatican. This policy, along with his actions against those members of the Catholic Theology Faculty at Bonn University who favoured a policy of conciliation with the government, led to his arrest on 20 November 1837 and his internment without trial. He was not released until 1840.

The publication which brought the incident to public attention, *Athanasius*, an accomplished work of modern journalism and rhetoric, which firmly advocated the concept of *Kirchenfreiheit* — that is a Church free from secular interference — was the first great document of German political Catholicism. It was written by Joseph Görres, journalist, political activist and Professor of History at the Ludwig-Maximilian University of Munich, of whom it was said following his death that he "would have become even greater than O'Connell, if there had been room for an O'Connell in Germany".[5]

Görres was the key figure in the influential group of Catholic theologians and philosophers, known as the Görres Circle, who, although holding a very conservative theological outlook, had progressive views on the issue of church-state relations and on the social questions of the day. The Görres family home in Munich was an important meeting place for Catholic intellectuals from Germany and abroad.

Moreover, Joseph Görres was not only interested in the state of Catholicism in Germany; he was also well aware of the condition of the Church in other countries. This led him, like many of his contemporaries, to be concerned about what was happening in Ireland. O'Connell is discussed by Görres in his personal correspondence and in a number of published articles. For him it was O'Connell's organisational skills which were particularly important, especially since a growing desire to set up some sort of Catholic association in Germany in the 1840s became evident. In Görres' eyes O'Connell was like a reaper who had brought new life to Ireland. "O'Connell," he wrote, "was merely sent to bind the sheaves and he has fulfilled this task with honour."[6]

A more critical view of O'Connell was taken by another member of the Görres Circle, the theologian Ignaz von Döllinger, who himself had contacts with a number of Irish scholars in Maynooth and who was an admirer of Archbishop John MacHale of Tuam, an important supporter of O'Connell. Döllinger disapproved of O'Connell's Repeal campaign, mainly because of his fear of the revolutionary potential of popular mass movements. His attitude towards O'Connell resulted in strained relations between him and the other members of the Circle. Nonetheless, Döllinger, who like Görres was a close friend of Montalembert, a man whose support of O'Connell is well known, did recognise O'Connell and his organisation as providing the best blueprint for a Catholic association.[7]

This conviction led to his involvement in 1848 in the development of a German Catholic organisation based on O'Connell's Catholic Association in Ireland, prior to his return to a full-time academic career in 1850. He believed that the German organisation should be spread throughout Germany and Austria and should help politicise German Catholics as a determined, cohesive force.

Another prominent German Catholic who held similar views was the Professor of Political Science and Law at the University of Freiburg, Franz Josef Ritter von Buss, who was based in Baden and was hailed as the "German O'Connell". Although Baden had a constitution and the reputation for being a liberal state, the administration had a definite anti-Catholic bias. It was Buss who led the movement against this, speaking against religious discrimination in the Baden Second Chamber in 1846 and putting his arguments in print. In many of his published works O'Connell figures prominently. Buss was obviously deeply impressed by O'Connell and his achievements. In his 1851 work *Die Aufgabe des katholischen Theils deutscher Nation in der Gegenwart, oder der katholische Verein Deutschlands* (which was dedicated to O'Connell) the exemplary importance of O'Connell's organisational and tactical skills for Buss is evident. In this and in other works Buss reveals his belief in the need to form associations on the model of that established by O'Connell in Ireland in the 1820s. For Buss the situation in Ireland, where the Church of the majority was oppressed by the Protestant authorities, mirrored that of the Catholic Church in the majority of states of the German Confederation, most notably in Prussia. Thus the success of the Irish struggle under O'Connell was one of the best examples Germans could have. In this work Buss readily acknowledged that he had adopted many of O'Connell's tactics in his own political career. Besides actively encouraging Catholics to send petitions to parliament, he also staged large open-air meetings reminiscent of O'Connell's dramatic "monster-meetings", a strategy he urged the Katholischer Verein Deutschlands to adopt.[8]

This organisation was founded in Mainz in 1848 as the Piusverein für religiöse Freiheit by the theologian, Adam Franz Lennig. Based in Mainz, one of the main centres of Catholic revival in the 1840s, Lennig had studied in France where he had established contact with French Liberal Catholic leaders — and through them received information on O'Connell, a fact which was to be of vital significance for the future development of the Katholischer Verein — and also had close links with members of the Görres Circle in Munich. In common with Buss and O'Connell, Lennig recognised the need to influence public opinion and was involved in the establishment of a number of Catholic journals. Moreover, he too was also influenced by O'Connell's tactics in Ireland, especially that of forming associations. When the law granting freedom of association was introduced in 1848, Lennig drew strongly on O'Connell's movement in

Ireland when he founded the Piusverein, the inaugural meeting of which was held on 23 March in Mainz. From an original membership of twenty-four, the organisation grew until in the area of Mainz alone there were over 400 members.[9] Soon branches of the organisation were being established all over Germany, and in October of that year the first general assembly was held.

It was at this first general assembly that the significant influence of O'Connell on the organisation and development of German political Catholicism becomes particularly evident. The title of the organisation was changed to one similar to O'Connell's Catholic Association in Ireland — to the Katholischer Verein Deutschlands. It was decided to adopt the policy of collecting a membership fee each month, payable at any of the weekly meetings — in direct imitation of O'Connell's Catholic Rent, a policy which was widely known and approved of by the German Catholic press.[10] Moreover, addresses to the people were to be issued — a policy adopted by O'Connell throughout his political career — and, again drawing on O'Connell for inspiration, newspapers and reading rooms were to be established and exploited as a way of influencing public opinion, politicising the people and mobilising them to agitate for the rights of the Church. Indeed at the first general assembly of the Katholischer Verein the vice-president of the organisation, the lawyer, Hardung, from Cologne, directly referred his listeners to O'Connell as the example to be followed closely:

> We no longer live in an era where miracles are a common occurrence, yet a miracle has taken place before our very eyes. In Ireland there is Daniel O'Connell, a man, who by keeping within the rules of law, is leading his people to freedom.[11]

This sentiment was reiterated by Buss, the elected first president of the organisation, in his popular work, *Der Kampf der Kirche gegen den Staat um ihre Freiheit in Frankreich und in Deutschland*, which was published in 1850.

Like O'Connell, the leaders of the Katholischer Verein stressed that their movement was not designed to damage the Protestant churches in any way. Moreover, like O'Connell, they also urged their members to demonstrate total loyalty to the Crown. Indeed throughout the 1840s the German Catholic press made constant reference to the fact that O'Connell successfully demonstrated how a devout Catholic could also be the loyal subject of a Protestant monarch, thereby removing the stigma of sedition previously attached to Catholics. In addition, the leaders of the Katholischer Verein also realised, as O'Connell had in the 1820s, that the support of key members of the episcopate was essential to their movement. Indeed, although a layman held the post of president, the general leadership of the organisation was dominated by members of the clergy, a situation which developed primarily because of the lack of suitable lay-men. Nonetheless, the Katholischer Verein was essentially lay in character and, unusually, it was pressure from their flock which forced the clergy to become involved — a striking parallel to the situation in Ireland in relation to O'Connell's organisations, as Fergus O'Ferrall points out in his excellent work *Catholic Emancipation: Daniel O'Connell and the Birth of Irish Democracy, 1820-30.*

Unlike O'Connell's movements, however, the Katholischer Verein Deutschlands never evolved into a major, popular movement. Nor was it directly involved in politics — though where the rights of the Church were under threat, political action was encouraged. Buss had originally planned to turn the organisation into a political party, in the belief that only a politically-motivated Catholic movement could improve the fortunes of the Church. In this as in many of his other strategies, O'Connell's example was a motivating factor. While this never formally took place, many prominent politicians were attracted to the movement. Among them was the future Bishop of Mainz, Wilhelm Emmanuel von Ketteler (1811-77), one of the most influential men in the nineteenth-century German Church and a great admirer of O'Connell, and August von Reichensperger (1808-95), who, along with his brother Peter (1810-92), drew on O'Connell's examples in speeches to the Prussian parliament in the 1850s.

In considering the success of the Katholischer Verein Deutschlands at bringing about the political awakening of German Catholics and co-ordinating their efforts, their adoption of O'Connell's techniques, both organisational and propagandist, emerge as fundamental influences — confirming the popularity of the view of O'Connell as the successful defender of the rights of the Irish Catholics among their German co-religionists. Yet following the successful establishment of the German Catholic association in 1848, the importance of the Irishman for German Catholics in general seems to have diminished. He had served his purpose by offering them the confidence to agitate against anti-Catholic state authorities and by providing them with the blueprint for practical action. His symbolic importance was stated clearly in the entry on the Liberator in the first edition of the Catholic lexicon, the *Allgemeine Realencyclopädie oder Conversationslexikon für das katholische Deutschland*, published by Manz in 1847:

> This great man, this champion of an oppressed people was one of the greatest men of all times. For, if the greatness of a man is judged on the beneficial influence he exerts on other people and through them on posterity, there has scarcely been a man, from any period or race, to compare with him.

His value for German Catholics in those times of difficulty prior to 1848 is reflected in their return to O'Connell's policies during the *Kulturkampf* in the 1870s. 1872 saw the foundation of the short-lived Mainzer Verein Deutscher Katholiken, again based on the Irish Catholic Association of the 1820s.[12] In 1875 Buss, in his last public speech, given at the general assembly of the Katholischer Verein in Freiburg, appealed to German Catholics not to forget O'Connell's example.[13] Thus O'Connell can justifiably be considered as one of the fundamental influences which resulted in the political awakening of German Catholicism in the nineteenth century. The sentiments expressed in the replies of the German Catholics invited by the O'Connell Centenary Committee to attend celebrations in Dublin in 1874 to mark the centenary of his birth are further evidence of this, the reply from August Reichensperger being a case in point:

> If in any way I deserve this honour it is for the admiration I felt since my youth for the Liberator of a nation destined to be a model and a source of comfort to all Catholics suffering persecution.[14]

NOTES AND REFERENCES

2. O'CONNELL AND THE MAKING OF IRISH POLITICAL CULTURE

1. Tom Garvin, "Defenders, Ribbonmen and Others: Underground Political Networks in Pre-Famine Ireland", in Charles H.E. Philpin, ed., *Nationalism and Popular Protest in Ireland* (Cambridge University Press, 1987), pp. 219-44.

2. National Archives, Washington, D.C., Despatches from U.S. Consuls at Dublin, Roll I, Vol. 1, 2 November 1791.

3. Jeffrey Praeger, *Building Democracy in Ireland* (Cambridge University Press, 1986), pp. 185-6.

4. W. Torrens McCullagh, *Memoirs of Sheil* (London, 1865), I, pp. 184-5.

5. *Ibid.*, p. 187.

6. W.J. O'Neill Daunt, *Ireland and her Agitators* (Dublin, 1845), pp. 239-40.

3. MAKING NATIONS: O'CONNELL, RELIGION AND THE CREATION OF POLITICAL IDENTITY

Professor Maurice O'Connell and Professor Tom Garvin read earlier drafts of this paper. I am grateful for their comments and suggestions. I have not always agreed with their point of view, but have appreciated their interest in my argument. I would also like to acknowledge the comments made by Tina Neylon when she read an earlier draft. Notwithstanding this help, I am entirely responsible for the argument and content of the article.

1. A Munster Farmer, *A Letter to Daniel O'Connell Esq. occasioned by the Petition adopted at the Late Aggregate Meeting of the Catholics of Ireland* (Dublin, 1824), p. 1. The author was Denys Scully, see Brian MacDermot (ed.), *The Catholic Question in Ireland and England: The Papers of Denys Scully* (Dublin, 1988), p. xx. Hereafter *Scully Papers*.

2. Anthony Giddens, *The Nation State and Violence* (Cambridge, 1985), p. 11: "To be an agent is to be able to make a difference to the world, and to be able to make a difference is to have power (where power means

transformative capacity)." See also R.G. Collingwood, *An Essay on Meta-physics* (Oxford, 1940).

3. Oliver MacDonagh, *The Hereditary Bondsman: Daniel O'Connell 1775-1829* (London, 1988), p. 94; John O'Connell (ed.), *The Life and Speeches of Daniel O'Connell, MP* (Dublin, 1846), I, pp. 22-3.

4. O'Connell to Hunting Cap, 3 January 1797, Maurice O'Connell (ed.), *The Correspondence of Daniel O'Connell* (Shannon: Irish University Press, 1972), I, p. 30.

5. O'Connell to Hunting Cap, 24 January 1797, *ibid.*, p. 32.

6. Kennedy F. Roche, "Revolution and Counter-Revolution" in Michael Tierney (ed.), *Daniel O'Connell* (Dublin, 1949); A. Houston (ed.), *Daniel O'Connell: Early Life and Journal* (London, 1906). O'Connell to Hunting Cap, 1 March 1798, *O'Connell Correspondence*, I, pp. 32-3.

7. Denys Scully, *An Irish Catholic's Advice to his Brethren...* (Dublin, 1803), p. 50.

8. John O'Connell (ed.), *op. cit.*, I, pp. 34-52 for speech. British is used to include those who live on the island of Britain and who acknowledge the legitimacy of the British state. For the most part it does not include the Irish whether Catholic or Protestant, though there is a sense in which the Protestant Irish become British later in the century.

9. E.J. Hobsbawm, *Nations and Nationalism since 1780* (Cambridge, 1990), p. 84.

10. In the United Kingdom the emergence of loyalist patriotism in reaction to the French Revolution is one case, as is the identity between the Catholic masses and legitimism in Spain. In Ireland and Belgium nationalism challenged the state structure and broke with its confines and authority.

11. J. Armstrong, *Nations Before Nationalism* (Chapel Hill, 1982); Benedict Anderson, *Imagined Communities* (London, 1983). By modern I mean the period of European history framed by the Enlightenment, the Industrial Revolution and the French Revolution. Despite Tom Garvin's best efforts to persuade me otherwise I remain convinced that there was considerable fluidity during this time. However, I recognise that it was short lived and did not realise its modernist potential.

12. Hobsbawm, *op. cit.*; A.D. Smith, *The Ethnic Origins of Nationalism* (Oxford, 1986).

13. Isaiah Berlin, "Joseph de Maistre and the Origins of Fascism" in *New York Review of Books*, 27 September, 11 and 25 October 1990 for an assessment.

14. Hobsbawm, *op. cit.*, p. 86.

15. W. Bagehot, *Physics and Politics* (London, 1887); J.S. Mill, *Representative Government* (London, 1861).

16. W.E.H. Lecky, *Democracy and Liberty* (London, 1896), p. 463.

17. Hobsbawm, *op. cit.*, p. 70.

18. N. Canny, "The Formation of the Irish Mind: Religion, Politics and Gaelic Irish Literature 1580-1750", *Past and Present*, No. 95 (May 1982), pp. 91-116. Canny implies that 1719 was the last hope for a Pretender in Ireland. However, this should not disguise the fact that the Irish Catholic masses remained committed to a sectarian anti-Protestant politics, though the other classes moved towards constitutionalism.

19. C.M. O'Keefe, *Life and Times of Daniel O'Connell* (Dublin, 1864), I, pp. 93-4; Hunting Cap to O'Connell, 14 December 1813, *O'Connell Correspondence*, pp. 346-7; MacDonagh, *op. cit.*, pp. 97-100.

20. Marianne Elliott, *Wolfe Tone: Prophet of Irish Independence* (New Haven

and London, 1989).

21. Bernard Ward, *The Eve of Catholic Emancipation* (London, 1911), I, pp. 74-80.
22. Owen Chadwick, *The Popes and the European Revolution* (Oxford, 1981).
23. Denis Gwynn draws attention to the theoretical objections to any interference in a church by a state. He adds, however, that in reality it was not an uncommon practice concluding that "...in Pitt's time there was good reason to believe that even a Protestant King in England could, in return for certain concessions and active assistance, expect to receive the same negative power of veto over the appointment of bishops which other non-Catholic sovereigns already enjoyed". Denis Gwynn, *The Struggle for Catholic Emancipation* (London, 1928), pp. 143-44.
24. Pastoral letter, 26 April 1798, cited in Evelyn Bolster, *A History of the Diocese of Cork: From the Penal Era to the Famine* (Cork, 1989), pp. 161-64, 168.
25. *Ibid.*, p. 169.
26. Denys Scully to Major Richard Huddleston, 5 March 1801, in *Scully Papers*, pp. 48-9; Scully to Earl of Hardwicke, 26 July 1803, pp. 67-8.
27. Scully, *An Irish Catholic's Advice...*, p. 51.
28. Circular to Irish hierarchy by Archbishop Troy, 29 May 1802.
29. Hobsbawm, *op. cit.*, pp. 46-79 for the non-nationalist antecedents which contribute to the elaboration of a nationalist ideology.
30. A Munster Farmer, *Reminiscences of Daniel O'Connell* (London and Dublin, 1847), p. 19.
31. Cited in Ward, *op. cit.*, II, pp. 145-6.
32. *Ibid.*, I, pp. 76-82.
33. Oliver MacDonagh, "The Politicization of the Irish Catholic Bishops: 1800-1850", *The Historical Journal*, xvii, 1 (1975), pp. 37-53, citation at p. 38.
34. Bolster, *op. cit.*, pp. 120-26 for an account of this incident.
35. Hobsbawm, *op. cit.*, p. 109; Anderson, *op. cit.*, deals with this question in detail.
36. In so far as rural Ireland was involved in the controversy the most systematic response came from the wealthier regions in the east of the country. I hope to analyse these and other dimensions of the controversy in the course of research on the middle classes and the rise of Irish nationalism.
37. Thomas Wyse, *Historical Sketch of the Late Catholic Association of Ireland* (London, 1829), I, p. 183.
38. *Ibid.*, p. 171.
39. Ward, *op. cit.*, I, pp. 79-80. Scully to Butler; Milner to Scully, 17 September 1808; Milner to Scully, 15 January 1809 in *Scully Papers*, pp. 171-3, 175-6, 184-5. Bolster, *op. cit.*, for Cork hostility to it.
40. Keogh to O'Connell, 12 February 1810; O'Connell to Edward Jerningham, c. mid-February 1810 in *O'Connell Correspondence*, I, pp. 210-11; Scully to Sir John Throckmorton, 6 April 1810; Milner to Scully, 20 December 1810; T. Finn to Scully, 16 March 1810 in *Scully Papers*, pp. 221-2, 257-9, 220.
41. Ward, *op. cit.*, I, pp. 141-50. Edward Jerningham wrote to Throckmorton referring to "The frenzy of religious and political fanaticism is now raging in Ireland to a degree I cannot make you fully sensible of...", 28 February 1810 in *Scully Papers*, p. 260.
42. Gwynn, *op. cit.*, p. 163.
43. Thomas Moore, *A Letter to the Roman Catholics of Dublin* (Dublin, 1810), p. 36.

44. Brendan Clifford (compiler), *The Veto Controversy* (Belfast and Cork, 1985), for an extensive review of the literature.
45. O'Keefe, *op. cit.*, I, pp. 418-19.
46. MacDonagh, *Hereditary Bondsman*, pp. 105-9.
47. Isaiah Berlin, *Four Essays on Liberty* (Oxford, 1969); Dudley Seers, *The Political Economy of Nationalism* (Oxford, 1983).
48. Mary O'Connell to O'Connell, 21 March 1809 in *O'Connell Correspondence*, I, pp. 193-94; Mary O'Connell to O'Connell, 11 March 1816 in *O'Connell Correspondence*, II, p. 85. MacDonagh, *Hereditary Bondsman*, pp. 100-101 believes that O'Connell was still "infervent" if not precisely "lukewarm" about religion when this letter was written.
49. Gwynn, *op. cit.*, pp. 165-67; Ward, *op. cit.*, II, pp. 23-56; MacDonagh, *Hereditary Bondsman*, p. 113; *Scully Papers*, pp. 423-37 for correspondence on the issue.
50. Sir Henry Parnell to Scully, 17 May 1817 in *Scully Papers*, pp. 618-20.
51. Chadwick, *op. cit.*, pp. 487-519, 527-28, 541ff. I am grateful to Professor Maurice O'Connell for alerting me to the importance of the Napoleonic Concordat.
52. Gwynn, *op. cit.*, p. 182; MacDonagh, *Hereditary Bondsman*, pp. 112-16; Milner to Scully, 21 May 1813; 4 June 1813 in *Scully Papers*, pp. 456, 460-62.
53. O'Connell to Mary O'Connell, 1 January 1813 in *O'Connell Correspondence*, I, p. 340.
54. John O'Connell (ed.), *op. cit.*, II, pp. 7-27; O'Keefe, *op. cit.*, I, pp. 272-73; Bolster, *op. cit.*, p. 215.
55. O'Keefe, *op. cit.*, I, pp. 391-97. For Dromgoole's speeches and a defence of his position, see Thomas Dromgoole, *The Speeches of Doctor Dromgoole, against surrendering the Government of the Catholic Church in Ireland to the Discretion of Parliament* (Dublin, 1814), pp. 31-5, 42-9.
56. O'Keefe, *op. cit.*, I, pp. 49-63 for the speeches.
57. Ward, *op. cit.*, II, *passim* for extensive discussion of these issues.
58. *Ibid.*, pp. 145-46.
59. Moylan to Milner, 7 December 1814, cited in Bolster, *op. cit.*, p. 218.
60. Parnell to O'Connell, 22 May 1815; O'Connell to Parnell, 31 May 1815; O'Connell to Parnell, 13 June 1815 in *O'Connell Correspondence*, II, pp. 37-41, 47.
61. Parnell to Scully, 10, 13, 17 May 1817 in *Scully Papers*, pp. 616-20.
62. For Northern Irish Protestant reaction, David Miller, *The Queen's Rebels* (Dublin, 1978); for the impact of the tithe agitation, Desmond Bowen, *The Protestant Crusade in Ireland* (Dublin, 1977), pp. 156-76. For an intriguingly hostile account of O'Connell's attempt to extend the Repeal Association to Northern Ireland, *The Repealer Repulsed* (Belfast, 1841).
63. MacDonagh, *Hereditary Bondsman*, pp. 217-20. An Irish Catholic, *The Voice of Ireland, Past and Present Against Pensioning the Irish Clergy* (Dublin, 1825), where O'Connell is quoted against the very position he was then taking.
64. O'Connell to Bishop Doyle, 29 December 1827 in *O'Connell Correspondence*, III, pp. 372-3.
65. O'Connell to Cullen, 9 May 1842 in *O'Connell Correspondence*, VII, pp. 155-60.

4. LIBERTY AND CATHOLIC POLITICS 1790-1990

1. Saint Augustine, *Confessions* (Penguin Books, London, 1961), Book XI. No. 20.
2. J. Lee, *Ireland 1912-1985: Politics and Society* (Cambridge University Press, 1989), pp. 586-97.
3. Gordon Wright, "History as a Moral Science", *The American Historical Review*, Vol. 81, No. 1, February 1976, pp. 8-9.
4. See R.F. Foster, "Varieties of Irishness" in *Cultural Traditions in Northern Ireland*, ed. M. Crozier (Institute of Irish Studies, QUB, 1989), p. 22.
5. J. Lee, "Grattan's Parliament" in *The Irish Parliamentary Tradition*, ed. Brian Farrell (Dublin, 1973), p. 156.
6. See Liam de Paor, "The Rebel Mind: Republican and Loyalist" in *The Irish Mind: Exploring Intellectual Traditions*, ed. R. Kearney (Dublin, 1985), pp. 167, 186-7 and O. MacDonagh, *States of Mind: A Study of Anglo-Irish Conflict 1780-1980* (London, 1983), pp. 72, 89.
7. Brian Farrell, "The Paradox of Irish Politics" in *The Irish Parliamentary Tradition*, pp. 21, 24.
8. For these models of response see especially Jeffrey Praeger, *Building Democracy in Ireland: Political Order and Cultural Integration in a Newly Independent Nation* (Cambridge University Press, 1986); for how deep-rooted these divergent approaches to the Irish past are, see the excellent article by Jacqueline R. Hill, "Popery and Protestantism, Civil and Religious Liberty: The Disputed Lessons of Irish History 1690-1812", *Past and Present*, No. 118, February 1988, pp. 96-129.
9. See Conor Cruise O'Brien, *The Siege: The Saga of Israel and Zionism* (Paladin, Grafton Books, London, 1988), pp. 653-655.
10. O. MacDonagh, *The Hereditary Bondsman: Daniel O'Connell 1775-1829* (London, 1988), pp. 41-2.
11. O. MacDonagh, "The Contribution of O'Connell" in *The Irish Parliamentary Tradition*, p. 165.
12. O'Connell in Tralee in 1818, quoted in M.R. O'Connell, *Daniel O'Connell: The Man and His Politics* (Dublin, 1990), p. 34.
13. Foreword, *ibid.*, p. 8.
14. *The Correspondent*, 5 March 1807.
15. O'Connell to Goldsmid, 11 September 1829 in *The Correspondence of Daniel O'Connell*, ed. M.R. O'Connell, Volume IV, Letter 1604.
16. *The Times*, 10 March 1831.
17. 10 March 1837, *Mirror of Parliament*, 1837, II, p. 594.
18. See F. O'Ferrall, "Daniel O'Connell and Henry Cooke: the conflict of civil and religious liberty in modern Ireland", *The Irish Review*, No. 1, 1986, pp. 20-27.
19. For the development of liberal Catholicism see V. Conzemius, "The Place of Daniel O'Connell in the Liberal Catholic Movement of the Nineteenth Century" and H. Rollet, "The Influence of O'Connell's Example on French Liberal Catholicism" in *The World of Daniel O'Connell*, ed. D. McCartney (Dublin, 1980), pp. 143-149, 150-162; see also R.F.B. O'Ferrall, "The Growth of Political Consciousness in Ireland 1823-1847: A Study of O'Connellite Politics and Political Education" (Ph.D. thesis, TCD, 1978), Part One, Ch. 3, "The Emergence of a Political Ideology: Irish Liberal Catholicism 1800-30".
20. See Gladstone in debate of 26 April 1883, Hansard, 3rd Series, CCLXXVIII, pp. 1190-91 and W.E. Gladstone, "Daniel O'Connell", *The Nineteenth*

Century, XXV, 1889.
21. B. Farrell, "The Paradox of Irish Politics" in *The Irish Parliamentary Tradition*, p. 23.
22. T.W. Moody, *Davitt and Irish Revolution 1846-82* (Clarendon Press, Oxford, 1982), p. 552.
23. *Glasgow Herald*, 25 March 1883, quoted in Moody, *Davitt and Irish Revolution 1846-82*, pp. 554-5.
24. M. Davitt, *The Fall of Feudalism in Ireland* (London, 1904), p. 35.
25. T. Garvin, "Priests and Patriots: Irish Separatism and Fear of the Modern, 1890-1914", *Irish Historical Studies*, XXV, No. 97, 1986, pp. 67-81.
26. T. Garvin, *The Evolution of Irish Nationalist Politics* (Dublin, 1981), p. 207.
27. T. Brown, *Ireland: A Social and Cultural History 1922-1985* (Fontana, London, 1985), p. 66.
28. See B. Farrell, "MacNeill in Politics" in *The Scholar Revolutionary: Eoin MacNeill, 1867-1945 and the Making of the New Ireland*, ed. F.X. Martin and F.J. Byrne (Dublin, 1973), p. 185.
29. See S. Ó Faoláin, *King of the Beggars* (London, 1938); M. Tierney, "Politics and Culture: Daniel O'Connell and the Gaelic Past", *Studies*, Vol. XXVII, No. 107, 1938, pp. 361-2; and Brown, *op. cit.*, pp. 155-8.
30. *Ibid.*, p. 205.
31. T. Garvin, "The Politics of Denial and of Cultural Defence: the Referenda of 1983 and 1986 in context", *The Irish Review*, No. 3, 1988, pp. 1-7.
32. S. Deane, "Edmund Burke and the Ideology of Irish Liberalism", in *The Irish Mind: Exploring Intellectual Traditions*, ed. R. Kearney (Dublin, 1985), p. 141.
33. Ó Faoláin, *The Irish*, pp. 103, 162.
34. W.M. Abbott, SJ (ed.), *The Documents of Vatican II* (London, 1967), p. 673.
35. L. McRedmond, "Sweet Liberty" in *Freedom to Hope? The Catholic Church in Ireland Twenty Years after Vatican II*, ed. A. Falconer, E. McDonagh, S. MacReamoinn (Dublin, 1985), p. 75.
36. See Alan D. Falconer (ed.), *Reconciling Memories* (Dublin, 1988), p. 4.
37. Governor Mario M. Cuomo, "Religious Belief and Public Morality: A Catholic Governor's Perspective", paper delivered to Department of Theology at the University of Notre Dame, 13 September 1984.
38. Lee, *Ireland 1912-1985: Politics and Society*, p. 633.

5. THE IMAGE IN ENGLAND: THE CARTOONS OF HB

1. Relatively little work has been done on nineteenth-century caricatures. The most directly relevant for this paper has been L.P. Curtis, Jr, *Apes and Angels: The Irishman in Victorian Caricature* (Washington, D.C., 1971); also helpful is his *The Anglo-Saxons and Celts: A study of Anti-Irish Prejudice in Victorian England* (Bridgeport, Conn., 1968). A recent effort to examine the image of an early nineteenth-century politician, largely through a study of the contemporary press, is Donald Read's *Peel and the Victorians* (Oxford, 1987). A special expression of gratitude for reading earlier versions of this paper and for many helpful suggestions is due to Maurice O'Connell, Professor Emeritus, Fordham University and Miles L. Chappell, Professor of Fine Arts, College of William and Mary.
2. Austin Dobson, "John Doyle", *Dictionary of National Biography*. No modern, scholarly study of Doyle exists. G.M. Trevelyan reprinted 62 of

Doyle's caricatures in 1952 with a seven page introduction, *The Seven Years of William IV: A Reign Cartooned by John Doyle* (London, 1952). See also Dorothy George, *English Political Caricature, 1793-1832* (Oxford, 1959), Vol. II, pp. 224-5 and ch. XIV.

3. Thomas MacLean, *An Illustrative Key to the Political Sketches of H.B. from no. 1 to no. 600* (London: M'Lean, 1841); *An Illustrative Key to the Political Sketches of H.B. from 601 to 800* (London: M'Lean, 1844). Abbreviated *Keys*, merely listing persons depicted, were issued for plates 1-887.

4. For an example of how Doyle could adapt a well-known painting to suit his own purposes, see: Miles L. Chappell and James N. McCord, Jr., "John Doyle, Daniel O'Connell, 'The Great Liberator', and Rubens: The Appropriate and Appropriation in Political Caricature", *Southeastern College Art Conference Review (SECAC)*, XI (1987), pp. 127-34.

5. Norman Gash, *Sir Robert Peel* (London, 1972), p. 689.

6. *The Letters of Thomas Babington Macaulay*, ed. by Thomas Pinney (Cambridge University Press, 1974), II, p. 64; *The Times*, 12 December 1834.

7. *The Times*, 11 August 1842.

8. *Morning Post*, 17 April 1839.

9. See J. Hungerford Pollen's Introduction to *A Journal Kept by Richard Doyle in the Year 1840* (London, 1886, 2nd ed.), p. v.

10. *Morning Post*, 20 November 1838.

11. [W.M. Thackeray], "Pictures of Life and Character by John Leech", *Quarterly Review*, XCVI (1854), pp. 75-86.

12. [W.M. Thackeray], "George Cruikshank", *Westminster Review*, XXXIV (June 1840), p. 4; [W.M. Thackeray], "Parisian Caricatures", *Westminster Review*, XXXII (April 1839), p. 160.

13. Philip H. Highfield, Jr, K.A. Burrin, and E.A. Langhe, *Biographical Directory of Actors, Actresses, Musicians, Dancers, Managers and Other Stage Personalities in London, 1660-1800* (Carbondale, 1978), Vol. 5, p. 59.

14. L.C. Sanders (ed.), *Lord Melbourne's Papers* (London, 1889), pp. 169-70, 173-4.

15. Angus Macintyre, *The Liberator: Daniel O'Connell and the Irish Party 1830-46* (London, 1965), p. 23.

16. See J.H. Whyte, "Daniel O'Connell and the Repeal Party", *Irish Historical Studies*, XI, No. 44 (September 1959), pp. 297-316.

17. Elie Halevy, *History of the English People in the Nineteenth Century* (London, 1927), III, p. 65.

18. Oliver MacDonagh, "Politics, 1830-45" in *A New History of Ireland: V, Ireland Under the Union; I, 1801-70*, ed. by W.E. Vaughan (Oxford, 1989), p. 173.

19. Macintyre, *The Liberator*, p. 46.

20. See MacLean's *Illustrated Key* (1841), p. 280, commenting on No. 418; Gerard J. Lyne, "Daniel O'Connell, Intimidation and the Kerry Election of 1835", *Journal of the Kerry Archaeological and Historical Society* (1971), pp. 86-7.

21. The *Key* lists Howick, Spring Rice and Russell in the pouch, but *The Illustrated Key* (1841) puts Glenelg in place of Howick, p. 253.

22. For O'Connell's finances and the origin of the O'Connell rent, see Oliver MacDonagh, *The Hereditary Bondsman: Daniel O'Connell, 1775-1829* (London, 1988), pp. 175-6.

23. *Illustrated Key*, pp. 279-80.

24. *The Times*, 9 April 1835.

25. *The Times*, 16 May 1835.

26. *The Times*, 17 November 1835.
27. See, for example, Mary Gordon, *Stereotype of Imagery and Belief* (Cambridge, England, 1962).
28. *The Times*, 26 March 1836.
29. Quoted in Angus Macintyre, *The Liberator*, pp. 155-8.
30. *Correspondence of Lord Aberdeen and Princess Lieven*, ed. by E. Jones Parry (London, 1938), p. 34.
31. *The Times*, 10 July 1835.
32. See Abraham D. Kriegel, "The Politics of the Whigs in Opposition, 1834-35", *The Journal of British Studies*, VII (1968), pp. 65-91; A.H. Graham, "The Lichfield House Compact", *Irish Historical Studies*, XII (1961), pp. 209-25; also Kriegel, "Irish Policy of Lord Grey's Government", *Historical Journal*, LXXXVI (1971), pp. 22-45.
33. See Kriegel (1968), Graham (1961), and Ian D.C. Newbould, "Whiggery and the Dilemma of Reform", *Bulletin of the Institute of Historical Research*, XII (1976), pp. 209-41. Also Richard Brent, *Liberal Anglican Politics: Whiggery, Religion and Reform 1830-41* (Oxford, 1987), ch. 2. Brent argues that the Whigs, independently of O'Connell and immediate party gain, were committed to reforming the Irish Church.
34. In addition to Newbould (1976), see Angus Hawkins, "Parliamentary Government and Victorian Political Parties, c.1830-c.1880", *English Historical Review*, CIV (July 1989), pp. 638-69.
35. I.D.C. Newbould, "Whiggery and the Growth of Party 1830-41: Organisation and the Challenge of Reform", *Parliamentary History*, 4 (1985), pp. 137-56.
36. Quoted in Macintyre, *The Liberator*, p. 157.
37. See Brent, *Liberal Anglican Politics*, esp. pp. 96-103.
38. Macintyre, *The Liberator*, p. 156.
39. Quoted in R.E. Foster, "Mr. Punch and the Iron Duke: Cartooning the Duke of Wellington", *History Today*, 34 (1984), pp. 36-42.
40. For patronage, see Macintyre, *The Liberator*, pp. 160-3.
41. *The Times*, 16 May 1835, referring to Nos. 391, 392 and 393.
42. *The Times*, 16 May 1835.
43. See Newbould (1976), p. 234.
44. According to Henry Lambert, MP for County Wexford, several politicians had approached Spring Rice about a motion for transferring the tithe to the landlords, but O'Connell had taken over the motion: "Thus, the insolent intrusion of this brazen ruffian caused the loss of this important amendment; it was evident the Lords would never sanction a measure proceeding from so foul and detestable a source." H. Lambert to Thomas Wyse, 16 October 1834, National Library of Ireland, Ms 15,025(3), Monteagle Papers.
45. Macintyre, *The Liberator*, p. 156.
46. Disraeli's Runnymede Letters, a series of nineteen published anonymously in *The Times* from 19 January 1836; quoted in Macintyre, *The Liberator*, p. 239.
47. *Blackwood's Magazine* XLIV (1838), p. 780.
48. *Morning Post*, 5 March 1838.
49. [W.M. Thackeray], "Parisian Caricatures", *Westminster Review*, XXXII (April 1839), p. 160.
50. Quoted in Macintyre, *The Liberator*, p. 157.
51. Quoted in *The History of The Times: The Thunderer in the Making, 1785-1841*, p. 370; Graham to Bonham, 2 January 1839.

52. Doyle to Peel, 11, 17 December 1841, 7, 22 January 1842; Peel to Doyle, 12 December 1841; British Library Add. Ms 40,497 ff. 116-20; 40,500 ff. 312-24 (Peel Papers).
53. Doyle to Peel, 22 January 1842, with memorandum attached, dated January 1842; B.L. Add. Ms 40,500 ff. 312-24 (Peel Papers).
54. Ibid.
55. Ibid.
56. *The Times*, 18 May 1844.
57. *The Times*, 21 August 1841.
58. In the autumn of 1835, Sir Frances Burdett attempted to have O'Connell expelled from Brooks's because of "ungentlemanly" language used in the north country tour. See HB's "High Bred and Low Bred" (No. 419, *Illustrated Key*, pp. 280-1).
59. See L.P. Curtis, Jr, *The Anglo-Saxons* and *Apes and Angels*.
60. Donald Southgate, *The Passing of the Whigs, 1832-86* (London, 1962), p. 61.

6. O'CONNELL IN IRISH FOLK TRADITION

Abbreviations
D.I.F.   Department of Irish Folklore, University College Dublin.
N.L.I.   National Library of Ireland.
P.R.   Private Recording in the author's possession.

1. Johann Georg Köhl, *Reisen in Irland*, 1843.
2. Recorded by Seán Ó Muirithe, Baile Mhúirne, Co. Cork, 1974. P.R.
3. Recorded by Seán Ó Muirithe, Baile Mhúirne, Co. Cork, 1974. P.R.
4. Cf. Caoimhín Ó Danachair, *Studia Hibernica*, 1974, p. 41; Lady Gregory, *Kiltartan History Book*, pp. 23-4; *Béaloideas*, XI, 1941, p. 125.
5. Recorded by Seán Ó Muirithe, Baile Mhúirne, Co. Cork, 1974. P.R.
6. Recorded by Seán Ó Muirithe, Baile Mhúirne, Co. Cork, 1974. P.R.
7. D.I.F. Vol. 858: Peig Sayers.
8. *Béaloideas*, XIV, 1944, pp. 106-7.
9. D.I.F. Vol. 125, p. 363; Vol. 126, p. 207; *An Claidheamh Soluis*, 16/8/1902.
10. D.I.F. Vol. 859, pp. 66-80.
11. Recorded by Seán Ó Muirithe, Baile Mhúirne, Co. Cork, 1974. P.R.
12. D.I.F. Vol. 125, p. 360.
13. Cf. Caoimhín Ó Danachair, *Studia Hibernica*, 1974, p. 52. The Irish sentence means: Daniel, how would you kill a pig at home?
14. D.I.F. Vol. 485, p. 148.
15. *Béaloideas*, XI, 1941, p. 116. This translation is by Seán Ó Súilleabháin, *The Folktales of Ireland*, London, 1966.
16. Recorded by Mrs Mary Sweeney, Meenbanad, Dungloe, Co. Donegal, 1960. P.R.
17. Pádraig Ó Míleadha, *Trí Glúine Gaedheal*, Dublin, 1953.
18. D.I.F. Vol. 308, p. 239.
19. Caoimhín Ó Danachair, *Studia Hibernica*, 1974, p. 64.
20. Recorded by Thomas Dee, Ardmore, Co. Waterford, 1974. P.R.
21. D.I.F. Vol. 304, p. 44.
22. In imitation of a famous epigram of Swift's, the poet Niall Sheridan composed the following, to add definition to a story concerning O'Connell's last will and testament. James Joyce was fond of quoting it:

Dying, he left his heart to Rome,
His testicles he left at home,
And showed by one satiric touch
No nation needed them so much.

23. *Amhráin Thomáis Rua*, ed. J. Fenton, Dublin, 1922.
24. Recited by Ríonach Ní Fhlathartaigh, D.I.F., 1974.
25. *Abhráin agus Dánta an Reachtabhraidh*, Dublin, 1933, ed. Douglas Hyde, p. 122.
26. Recited by Ríonach Ní Fhlathartaigh, D.I.F., 1974.
27. *Diarmuid na Bolgaighe agus a Chomharsain*, Seán Ó Súilleabháin, Dublin, 1933.
28. "Aisling", by Séamus Heaney. From *North*, Faber and Faber, London, 1975.
29. N.L.I.
30. Ibid.
31. Cf. *Ballads and the Law*, G. Ó Dúghaill, *Ulster Folklife*, XIX, 1973.
32. *Ibid.*
33. *Ibid.*
34. *Ibid.*
35. Recited by Frank Harte, Dublin, 1975. P.R.
36. Recited by Frank Harte, Dublin, 1975. P.R.
37. N.L.I.
38. Manuscript in the possession of Jack Devereux, Kilmore, Co. Wexford. The entire play is printed in *Irish Folk Drama*, Alan Gailey, Dublin, 1970.
39. N.L.I. Printed in *Songs of Irish Rebellion*, Zimmerman, Dublin, 1967, p. 231.
40. Cf. Pádraigh Ó Fiannachta, *Léas ar an Litríocht*, Dublin, 1975.
41. *Ibid.*

7. A RESONANT TRADITION: SOME GAELIC POETRY OF UÍBH RÁTHACH

Bolger, Dermot, *Internal Exiles* (Portlaoise, 1986).
Carney, James, *The Irish Bardic Poet* (Dublin, 1967).
Clarke, Austin, *Selected Poems* (Winston — Salem, 1976).
Graves, Robert, *The White Goddess* (London, 1953).
Kennelly, Brendan, ed., *The Penguin Book of Irish Verse* (Harmondsworth, 1981).
Kinsella, Thomas, *One* (Dublin, 1974).
Kinsella, Thomas, ed., *The New Oxford Book of Irish Verse* (Oxford, 1986).
Mac Réamoinn, Seán, ed., *The Pleasures of Gaelic Poetry* (London, 1982).
Montague, John, ed., *The Faber Book of Irish Verse* (London, 1974).
Ní Shúilleabháin, Máire, ed., *Amhráin Thomáis Rua Uí Shúilleabháin* (Máigh Nuad, 1985).
O'Brien, Flann, *At Swim-Two-Birds* (Harmondsworth, 1967).
O'Connell, M.J., *The Last Colonel of the Irish Brigade* (London, 1892).
O'Rahilly, Cecile, ed., *Five Seventeenth Century Political Poems* (Baile Átha Cliath, 1952).
Ó Tuama, Seán, ed., *Caoineadh Airt Uí Laoghaire* (Baile Átha Cliath, 1961).
Simmons, James, *Poems 1956-1986* (Dublin, 1986).

8. O'CONNELL, MONTALEMBERT AND THE BIRTH OF CHRISTIAN DEMOCRACY IN FRANCE

Daley, Rev G., "Montalembert and his visit to O'Connell" in *Catholic World*, 1900, T.LXXI, p. 331.

Foisset, Théophile, *Vie du R.P. Lacordaire* (Paris, Lecoffre fils, 2 vols., 1870).

Hogan, J., "Echos d'Irlande" in *Revue Montalembert*, Centenary Issue of 25 December 1910.

Lacordaire, *Éloge Funèbre de Daniel O'Connell prononcé à Notre Dame de Paris le 10 février 1848* (Paris, Sagnier et Bray, 1848).

Lamennais, abbé F. de, *Oeuvres Complètes* (Paris, Paul Daubrée et Cailleux, 1836-37).

Lamennais, abbé F. de, *Correspondance de Lamennais*, edited by Forgues (Paris, Paulin, 2 vols., 1859).

Lamennais, abbé F. de, *Lettres inédites de Lamennais à Montalembert*, edited by Forgues (Paris, Perrin, 1898).

Lecanuet, R.P., *Montalembert* (Paris, Pousielgue, 3 vols., 1895-1902).

Montalembert, *De l'Avenir Politique de l'Angleterre* (Paris, Didier, 1856), Chapter 10 on O'Connell.

Montalembert, *Les Moines d'Occident depuis Saint Benoit jusqu'à Saint Bernard* (Paris, Lecoffre, 7 vols., 1860-1877).

Montalembert, *Oeuvres, Discours 1831-1845* (Paris, Lecoffre, 9 vols., 1892); the "Lettre sur le Catholicisme en Irlande" is published in Volume 4, pp. 128-167.

O'Connell, Maurice, *Daniel O'Connell: The Man and his Politics*, with a foreword by Conor Cruise O'Brien (Dublin, Irish Academic Press, 1990).

Pauly, Marie-Hélène, *Les Voyageurs Français en Irlande au temps du Romantisme* (Paris, Gabriel Enault, 1939), Chapter VI on Montalembert.

Thureau-Dangin, *L'Eglise et l'Etat sous la Monarchie de Juillet* (Paris, Plon, 1880).

Trannoy, André, *Le Romantisme Politique de Montalembert avant 1843* (Paris, Bloud et Gay, 1942).

This paper was completed before the publication of two relevant studies was announced. They are:

Cattaneo, Bernard, *Montalembert: un Catholique en Politique* (Chambray, Editions C.L.D., 1990).

Montalembert, *Journal Intime Inédit*; text established, presented and annotated by Louis Le Guillou and Nicole Roger-Taillade (Paris, Editions du CNRS, 2 vols. [to be continued], 1990).

9. O'CONNELL AND GERMAN POLITICS

1. *Kölnische Zeitung*, 7 January 1840.
2. *Das Staatslexikon*, ed. by Carl von Rotteck and Carl Theodor Welcker, vol. 10 (Altona, 1848), p. 78 (entry "O'Connell", pp. 69-93).
3. Moritz Brühl, *Irland und O'Connell. Beiträge zur Kenntnis der neueren Geschichte Irlands. Nebst O'Connell's Prozeß. Zugleich als Fortsetzung von Irland's Zuständen in alter und neuer Zeit* (Regensburg, 1845). P. Duprat, *Daniel O'Connell, sein Leben und Wirken* (Leipzig, 1847). Anon., *Irland und die Repealfrage. Einige Worte über die Agitation O'Connells für die Aufhebung der Union zwischen Groß-britannien und Irland* (Leipzig, 1847). Anon., *O'Connell und sein Prozeß. Eine quellenmäßige Darstellung*

(Krefeld, 1844). See also L. Schipper, *Irland's Verhältnis zu England, geschichtlich entwickelt, und O'Connell's Leben und Wirken* (Soest, 1844); Jakob Venedey, *Irland*, 2 vols. (Leipzig, 1844) and Friedrich von Raumer, *England im Jahre 1835* (Leipzig, 1836), which also deals extensively with Ireland.

4. *Otto von Bismarck, Die gesammelten Werke*, vol. 14, 1: *Briefe*, ed. by Wolfgang Windelband and Werner Frauendienst (2nd edn. Berlin, 1933), p. 15.

5. Ernst Ludwig von Gerlach, *Aufzeichnungen aus seinem Leben und Wirken 1795-1877*, 1 (Schwerin, 1903), p. 351. Gerlach's visit to Dublin lasted from 17-20 August 1844.

6. "I said that we had come not to exchange opinions, but to listen and to learn, to which he did not reply. In the whole conversation there was no reference to politics or to his present circumstances... His bearing was polite, easy, distinguished, relaxed, like that of a grand gentleman who is used to having admirers presented to him and making small talk with them... I gave up hope of any serious conversation" (*ibid.*, pp. 394-5).

7. German publications on Ireland before 1830 are listed in Jürgen Schneider/Ralf Sotscheck, *Irland. Eine Bibliographie selbständiger deutschsprachiger Publikationen. 16. Jahrhundert bis 1989* (Darmstadt, 1988), pp. 283-286.

8. See Karl Holl, *Die irische Frage in der Ära Daniel O'Connells und ihre Beurteilung in der politischen Publizistik des Vormärz* (Mainz, 1958), p. 10, and the older study by Frieda Braune, *Edmund Burke in Deutschland. Ein Beitrag zur Geschichte des historisch-politischen Denkens* (Heidelberg, 1917).

9. J. W. von Goethe, *Conversations with Eckermann (1823-1832)*, translated by John Oxenford (San Francisco, 1984), pp. 255-6.

10. Anon., *England wider O'Connell, oder Der Weltprozeß* (Dortmund, 1844), pp. 1-9. The author was from Westphalia.

11. Hermann von Pückler-Muskau, *Briefe eines Verstorbenen. Ein fragmentarisches Tagebuch aus England, Wales, Irland und Frankreich, geschrieben in den Jahren 1828 und 1829* (Stuttgart, 1831). Rainer Gruenter, "Der reisende Fürst. Fürst Hermann Pückler-Muskau in England", in *Der curieuse Passagier. Deutsche Englandreisende des achtzehnten Jahrhunderts als Vermittler kultureller und technologischer Anregungen* (Heidelberg, 1983), pp. 119-137. Elizabeth Butler, *The Tempestuous Prince: Hermann von Pückler-Muskau* (London, 1929). Johann Georg Köhl, *Reisen in Irland* (Dresden and Leipzig, 1843).

12. For O'Connell's influence on German Catholicism see Geraldine Grogan's contribution in this volume and her book *The Noblest Agitator: Daniel O'Connell and the German Catholic Movement 1830-50* (Dublin, 1991).

13. The editor of the *Konstitutionelle Jahrbücher* (Stuttgart) on 30 October 1843, quoted in Angela Mickley, "Politischer Katholizismus und konstitutionelle Bewegung. Daniel O'Connells irischer Weg", Ph.D. thesis (Berlin, 1984), p. 209.

14. Robert Blum, *Politische Schriften*, 3 (Nendeln, 1979), part 2, p. 85.

15. *Kölnische Zeitung*, 8 December 1843

16. Friedrich Christoph Dahlmann, *Die Politik auf den Grund und das Maß der gegebenen Zustände zurückgeführt* (Leipzig, 1835), p. 72.

17. Quoted in K. Holl, p. 80.

18. See *ibid.*, pp. 28-9.

19. *Allgemeine Zeitung* (Augsburg), 1 October 1844 (quoted in K. Holl, p. 82).

20. See K. Holl, p. 83.

21. *Ibid.*
22. *Ibid.*
23. Reported in A. Mickley, p. 210.
24. Edgar Fleig (ed.), "Briefe Carl Ernst Jarckes an Legationsrat Dr. Moritz Lieber", in *Hochland* 18 (1920-21), pp. 730-1, 473.
25. Quoted in K. Holl, p. 61.
26. Anon., *Darstellung des gegenwärtigen Zustandes von Irland* (Stuttgart and Tübingen, 1835), quoted in K. Holl, p. 71.
27. See K. Holl, pp. 20, 62-3.

10. O'CONNELL'S IMPACT ON THE ORGANISATION AND DEVELOPMENT OF GERMAN POLITICAL CATHOLICISM

1. Joseph Görres (1776-1848) was a renowned Catholic journalist and Professor of History at the University of Munich. Ignaz von Döllinger (1799-1890) was Professor of Theology at the same university. Franz Josef Ritter von Buss (1803-78) was a politician and Professor of Political Science and Law at the University of Freiburg, and Adam Franz Lennig (1803-66) was a Catholic theologian based in Mainz. He later worked closely with the well-known Bishop of Mainz, Wilhelm Emmanuel von Ketteler.
2. The poems about O'Connell included Levin Schücking's "An Daniel O'Connell", Georg Weerth's "Gebet eines Irländers" and "Ein Sonntagabend auf dem Meere", along with Georg Günther's "Daniel O'Connell". Books written about O'Connell include Moritz Brühl's *Irland und O'Connell*, 2 vols. (Regensburg, 1845), Carl Rintel's *O'Connell's Process* (Münster, 1845) and Ludwig Schipper's *Irlands Verhältnis zu England geschichtlich entwickelt und O'Connells Leben und Wirken* (Soest, 1844). O'Connell also features largely in popular German travelogues on Ireland and Britain, among them Hermann von Pückler-Muskau's *Briefe eines Verstorbenen*, 4 vols. (Stuttgart, 1830-32), Friedrich von Raumer's *England im Jahre 1835*, 2 vols. (Leipzig, 1836) revised and enlarged edition in 3 vols. (Leipzig, 1842), Johann Georg Köhl's *Reisen in Irland*, 2 vols. (Dresden and Leipzig, 1844) and Jakob Venedey's *Irland*, 2 vols. (Leipzig, 1844).
3. *Allgemeine Zeitung*, 1 October 1844. Report originally published in the *Frankfurter O.P.A. Zeitung*.
4. Ernst Rudolf Huber, *Deutsch Verfassungsgeschichte seit 1789*, Vol. I (Stuttgart, 1957-81), p. 409.
5. *Der Katholik*, 4 March 1848.
6. This originally appeared in an article entitled "Der Gustav-Adolph-Verein und die irische Sache", in Vol. XIII of the *Historisch-politische Blätter* (1841) which is given in Vol. XVI of Wilhelm Schellberg / Adolf Dyroff *et al.*, *Joseph Görres: Gesammelte Schriften (im Auftrag der Görres Gesellschaft)*, 16 vols. (Cologne, 1926-39).
7. For Döllinger's approval of O'Connell's organisational policies see Vol. III, pp. 57f. of Johann Friedrich's *Ignaz von Döllinger. Sein Leben auf Grund seines schriftlichen Nachlasses*, 3 vols. (Munich, 1899-1901).
8. Buss, *Die Augfgabe...*, p. 446.
9. Bergsträsser Ludwig, *Studien zur Vorgeschichte der Zentrumspartei; Beiträge zur Parteigeschichte*, Vol. 1 (Tübingen, 1910), p. 148.
10. *Verhandlungen der ersten Versammlung des katholischen Vereines Deutschlands am 3., 4., 5. und 6. October zu Mainz* (Mainz, 1848), p. 84 and

Katholische Sonntagsblätter, 19 March 1848.
11. *Verhandlungen der ersten Versammlung des katholischen Vereines Deutschlands am 3., 4., 5. und 6. October zu Mainz* (Mainz, 1848), p. 15.
12. Margaret Anderson, *Windthorst: a political biography* (Oxford, 1981), p. 180.
13. Karl Buchheim, *Ultramontanismus und Demokratie. Der Weg der deutschen Katholiken im 19. Jahrhundred* (Munich, 1963), p. 268.
14. *O'Connell Centenary Record, 1875* (Dublin, 1878), p. 448, letter dated 6 July 1875.

INDEX